Thanks to Preetika Gupta, Suzanne Case
and Michael Grevis of the International
Association of Colour (iac@cix.xo.uk)

Thanks also to Apple UK PR for their help.

Important note on websites

We've done our very best to make sure that the online information listed in this book is as appropriate, accurate and up-to-date as possible at the time of going to press. However, information on the Internet is liable to change. Website addresses and website content are constantly being updated and sites occasionally close down. In addition, there is the possibility that some websites may contain material or links to material that is unsuitable for young people. Parents are strongly advised to ensure that access to the Internet is supervised by a responsible person.

The publishers cannot accept responsibility for any third party websites or any material contained in or linked to the same or for any consequences arising from use of the Internet.

Contents

Chapter 1: Imagine   1

Welcome to the iPod revolution

Chapter 2: Phenomenon   5

Classic or mini, from green to gold, the
choice is yours . . .

Chapter 3: Burn, Burn   19

Rip, mix, burn your music collection and
start creating playlists

Chapter 4: I Fought the Law   40

. . . and the law won. How to stay on the
right side of the rozzers

Chapter 5: Surfin' UK   50

The lowdown on downloading and the
best sites for legal music

Chapter 6: Together in Electric Dreams   64

Hello, is it me you're looking for? The iPod
puts you in touch

Chapter 7: More Than That   80

The iPod's not just for playing music,
you know

Chapter 8: She's in Fashion   96

All the best accessories from cases
to snowboard jackets

Chapter 9: Trouble   115

Ouch! What to do if your machine's
playing up

Chapter 10: Talking 'bout a Revolution   134

The next generation of iPods

my**Pod**

jeremy case

PUFFIN

PUFFIN BOOKS

Published by the Penguin Group
Penguin Books Ltd, 80 Strand, London WC2R 0RL, England
Penguin Group (USA), Inc., 375 Hudson Street, New York,
New York 10014, USA
Penguin Books Australia Ltd, 250 Camberwell Road,
Camberwell, Victoria 3124, Australia
Penguin Books Canada Ltd, 10 Alcorn Avenue, Toronto,
Ontario, Canada M4V 3B2
Penguin Books India (P) Ltd, 11 Community Centre,
Panchsheel Park, New Delhi – 110 017, India
Penguin Group (NZ), cnr Airborne and Rosedale Roads,
Albany, Auckland 1310, New Zealand
Penguin Books (South Africa) (Pty) Ltd, 24 Sturdee Avenue,
Rosebank 2196, South Africa

Penguin Books Ltd, Registered Offices: 80 Strand, London
WC2R 0RL, England

www.penguin.com

First published 2004
2

Thanks to the following companies for
permission to use images:
Pages 8, 9 and 13 (iPod and iPod mini) – Apple UK
Pages 96–114 Accessories – Altec Lansing,
tentechnology.com, haflkeyboard.com, marware.com

The moral right of the author has been asserted

Set in 9pt Chicago
Made and printed in England by Clays Ltd, St Ives plc

British Library Cataloguing in Publication Data
A CIP catalogue record for this book is available from the
British Library

ISBN 0-141-31905-4

Chapter 1   >

Imagine

Every song you've ever owned in the palm of your hand

The iPod has revolutionized the way we listen to music. It allows us to carry around anything from 1,000 to 10,000 tunes, so we can play out our lives to a constant soundtrack and tailor the music to our surroundings with the press of a button. No longer do we have to plan in advance what we want to listen to and lug around piles of CDs or MiniDiscs 'just in case'. Or stop the player on the bus or mid-jog and dig into our bag to change albums. We can hear what we want, when we want.

'Listening to music will never be the same again,' said iPod creator and Apple chief Steve Jobs. 'You can put your entire music collection in your pocket.' No wonder there are already 3 million (and counting) happy iPod owners.

With so much tuneage at your fingertips, suddenly you can approach even the most boring chores, like washing up or cleaning the car, with a smile on your face, knowing that your favourite band will be there to accompany you every step of the way. It's like a radio station that plays all your favourite music all the time with no ads or DJs who love the sound of their own voice. Now you call the shots. You can wrap yourself up snugly in your own musical comfort blanket and block out annoying everyday sounds like car alarms, road drills or your mum screaming at you to tidy up. Even if you do have to turn off for a second (well, we've all got to go to sleep sometime), when you switch your iPod back on, it starts playing from exactly where you left off.

Freed from the yawnsome boredom of everyday life, you can let your imagination run riot. Life before iPods seems like a silent movie compared to today's big budget action blockbuster. With those earbuds in, suddenly you're not just walking home, you're Frodo Baggins in *The Return of the King* on his epic journey towards Sauron's Mount Doom. You're not buying milk from the corner shop, you're James Bond on a top-secret dairy reconnaissance mission. Licensed to chill. It's like you're living your whole life in a movie with yours truly as the director.

But if you're not in the mood for calling the shots, why not let the iPod do the directing for you? Just switch to shuffle. Suddenly you get a mix that you'd never hear on the radio in a gadzillion years. Sometimes your iPod even seems to know what you were thinking as it throws up long-forgotten classics that fit perfectly with last week's most played track. The iPod has taught us that listening to our music collections isn't about albums any more. As any DJ knows, it's to do with mixing singles together to build up atmosphere and emotion. It's a musical journey with your iPod in the driving seat of a Ferrari and 40GB of extra horsepower purring underneath that beautiful hood. Because that's the other thing — they look so damn good too.

As soon as most of us get our iPod, we'll spend a couple of minutes admiring the gorgeous packaging before tearing the box open, charging up our new toy and loading it with our entire CD collection. But while we're doing it, we'll uncheck all those album fillers we never really listen to and realize we've still got a half-empty iPod. So we'll browse through our mates' music collections, discovering new bands, and tracks we'd never even heard of from our favourite artists. And then go online or down the high street to buy them. We'll wander around for the next few weeks in a completely new aural landscape until we've got music coming out of our ears.

But there's a reason why the iPod isn't simply called an iPlayer and why it's the number one MP3 player in the world - because it does way more than play music. In this book you'll discover that you can use your iPod to listen to books like the latest Harry Potter, store phone numbers and email addresses, have it send you to sleep at night, wake you up the next morning and let you know when that project's due in - and even actually store the work for you. You'll find out how to carry around digital photos on the iPod and record miniDiscs, tapes and vinyl, as well as college lectures and your mates' pathetic karaoke attempts. You'll find out which celebs are iPod lovers and meet the teens who got sued for downloading music off the Internet. You'll make sure it doesn't happen to you by checking out the huge legal digital music libraries at places like the iTunes Music Store UK - and even websites where they're giving away songs for free.

You'll find out how to use your iPod to DJ at special club nights or to pre-record entire party soundtracks so you can press play, leave it to do its thang and go off to mingle with other iPod lovers. Because when you buy an iPod, you'll realize that you've joined an exclusive club where anyone else wearing those white headphones becomes a potential new mate. Yes, the iPod actually makes the world a friendlier place and, if you're really lucky, can even find you love. What other MP3 player can do that?

iSay . . .

'I love my iPod. It changed my life completely.' Andy Schearer, Aberdeen

'The iPod is the Gucci of MP3.' Mike Maloney, Dublin

'I call it my fifth limb because it's really never off me.' Jonathan Eaton, Maryland, USA

myPod

Chapter 2 >

Phenomenon

How the little iPod made the big league. And then went stratospheric

The world has gone iPod crazy. A whopping 750,000 people across the world unwrapped an iPod for Christmas 2003 (jealous, us?). Just one London store was selling 300 a day in the run-up to the festive season and in the Apple Centre in Dublin, each new delivery of 140 iPods disappeared in twenty-four hours. One retailer said: 'They're like hot cakes. They come in and go out the same day.' For the first time, Apple was selling more iPods than its whole range of iMac computers put together.

It was a similar story when the iPod mini launched in the US in January 2004. There were round-the-block queues at Apple shops across New York, and 100,000 had been pre-ordered. It sold out within days - in every colour - and itchy-fingered customers were put on waiting lists of up to three months. Apple said that the problem was a shortage of Hitachi's one-inch hard drives and put back the mini's release in Europe for several months. Prices on ebay went crazy. In April 2004, when the minis were originally due to be released in the UK, one loaded (or stupid) punter bought a pink mini for £495 (nearly £100 more than a 40GB iPod!). Another pink one went for £380 and there were forty-four bids on a £280 blue. One guy even posted a message saying he knew how to find one and was selling this top-secret info to the highest bidder. If only we'd thought of that.

WE ARE FAMILY

From the who's-the-daddy 40GB to new arrival, the iPod mini

What makes the iPod different from all the other digital music players? It has an actual hard disk just like the ones you find on computers. So not only can you store entire days' more tunes, but also text files, contact details, calendars and even digital photos. The iPod also uses a 32MB memory cache with no moving parts, which in plain English means that you've got twenty-five minutes of non-skip play, so it's fine to go for a run or snowboarding while listening. We're not sure what would happen if you hit a tree, but then it's probably best not to find out. They're that rare combination of ground-breaking design and such simplicity that even your nan could play a few tunes. Compatible with Macs and PCs, iPods come with a CD containing the iTunes software, which works with Mac OS X v10.1.5 (v10.2.8 is recommended) or Windows 2000 or XP. If you have an older operating system, either upgrade (check www.amazon.co.uk) or download a free earlier version of iTunes for Mac OS 9 from http://docs.info.apple.com/article.html?artnum=120073. Windows users should install Musicmatch Jukebox Basic, free from www.musicmatch.com/download. Throughout the book we're assuming you read the iPod instructions while you were powering it up (remember to always charge it fully first time round, however eager you are to start using it). But if you accidentally ripped them up while you were tearing open the packaging, there are iPod tutorials on the Apple website (www.apple.com/support/ipod).

WHITE IPODS

All white with a chrome backside, the iPod is the size of a deck of playing cards, weighs less than two CDs (5.6oz or 6.2oz for the 40GB model) and fits easily in your palm so you can use it with one hand.

The hard disk on the 40GB model is actually more powerful than many PCs and holds 10,000 four-minute songs. It could keep you in tunes during a round-the-world trip - it takes four weeks of twenty-four-hour play before you hear the same tune twice - or surprise you with one new track every day for the next twenty-seven years. By which time you'll be middle-aged and much more interested in how

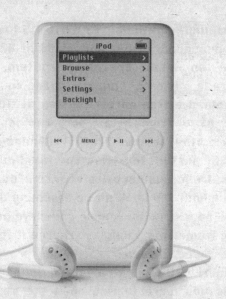

to get from Hull to Grimsby using the B546 back road than music. The 20GB iPod holds 5,000 songs (enough for 14 days) but doesn't come with a docking station. You can also find blue 40GB and 20GB iPods made by electronics giant, Hewlett Packard (called HP Digital Music Players). It's a sure sign of world domination when the world's number two computer-maker (and a Windows company!) is allowed to use Apple's brilliant design brain. As Steve Jobs said: 'Hell has frozen over!'

iSay . . .

'*I know this is stupid, but I loaded 2,000 songs on to my iPod and keep feeling it should weigh more with all those tunes packed into it. And yet, somehow it doesn't. Magic.*' Jon Casimir, Sydney, Australia

MINI IPODS

About the same size as a mobile phone but not as heavy, the mini's so ickle that you can slip it into your jeans pocket and not even notice. Be careful when you sit down, though, or you could be walking funny for days. The mini also comes in five cool colours - silver, gold, blue, pink and green. Made of stain-resistant anodized aluminium, its surface is fingerprint-proof and better at resisting scratches (the screen is slightly set back too). A third lighter (3.6oz) than the white iPods, the smaller size is popular with

sport nuts and people with tiny hands (keep it away from your kid brother). And the 4GB hard disk still has space for 1,000 four-minute songs, which is over sixty-six hours of solid listening. OK, so it copies files 3.5 times slower than a 40GB, but you probably won't even notice. The display is just as easy to read, but as the mini uses six lines of text rather than seven, it can't show album info when a song's playing. Because of a different font (Epsy vs Chicago, fact fans) and a smaller type, however, it actually boasts an extra letter width-ways. The mini comes with a belt clip and a USB 2.0 and FireWire cable, and can actually charge through the USB connection with your computer. Plus, when you plug in your earphones, it wakes up automatically. How considerate.

i'M a celebrity: Nitin Sawhney

'*I've just got the new iPod, which is amazing! Just the idea of having 1,000 tracks in your pocket is great.*'

iSay . . .

'*I bought a mini because I don't need all my music in one player - just enough so that when I travel, I'll have a few hours of music.*' Michelle Palmer, New York

'*There are certain things in life that are better small. This is one of them. All my friends have the bigger one - I want the best one.*' Kevin Lewis, New York

You What?

Jargon buster for technophobes

FLASH MEDIA
Most of the iPod's rivals (and digital cameras and the like) use Flash Media as their storage system as opposed to a hard disk. Flash players normally only store a couple of hours of music.

DIGITAL MUSIC
In the Dark Ages, music was recorded as analogue sound waves on vinyl and cassettes. Compact discs converted these waves into a stream of numbers for a higher quality recording that could be stored on a computer's hard disk in AIFF or WAV (PCs) format. AIFF and WAV files play on the iPod but you can squeeze way more on there by using compressed files like MP3 and AAC.

MP3
Digital MP3 tracks take up about ten per cent of the storage space of AIFF or WAV. The data is compressed, like zip files for text, and cuts out a lot of sounds that the human ear can't hear. These smaller files can be downloaded much more quickly from the Internet, leading to peer-to-peer swapping sites and the birth of legal online music stores.

AAC

Short for Advanced Audio Coding, the AAC format has better sound quality than MP3 and also takes up thirty to forty per cent less storage space. Developed by Dolby, Sony, Nokia et al, AAC supports surround sound and is the format used by the iTunes Music Store.

WMA

Windows Media Audio is the MP3 format used by, you guessed it, Windows-based PCs, and many legal music download sites. You can't play WMA files on the iPod, but it is possible to convert them (see Chapter Five) if they're not copy-protected.

COLOUR THE WORLD

What your ishade says about you

Pink and blue are going for the highest prices on ebay, Apple claim that silver and pink are the most popular, green is a hit in Hong Kong and gold - could it be the bling-bling option for wannabe hip-hopsters? Of course, what iPod colour you choose could simply come down to what they had left in the shop, hidden at the back of the store room, or whether it matched with the shirt you were wearing that day. But on the other hand, it could tell you a whole lot about your personality. The iPod as mind-reader? Is there no end to the little guy's talents?

SILVER

A bit of a gadget freak, you're drawn to shiny new technology like an electronic magpie. You're not a morning person but once you've dragged yourself out of that bed, you're very popular, good with people and bursting with enthusiasm. And you'll always be the first on the mobile - or text, email or MSN Messenger - to rave on about the latest hot new band. Or that track you've just made in your bedroom.

Typical owners: Daniel Bedingfield and June Sarpong

GOLD

Full of energy, you like your music to match your upbeat personality so tend to be into styles like dance, rock and rap. You're quite sporty and love outdoor activities - your favourite pastime would probably be beach volleyball. You're lively and entertaining and can be a bit of a show-off, but it's really a front because underneath you're quite a deep and spiritual person. Either that or a celebrity.

Typical owners: Kelis and Goldie (obviously)

BLUE

The most popular colour in the spectrum - and not just because of Levi's jeans. Blue shows you're a cool customer, who likes to take things easy and de-stress whenever you can. In fact, you're probably so attached to your iPod that your mates reckon your 'phones are an extension of your ears. What are you listening to? Dub reggae, soul and chillout music like Zero 7, natch. Some people might think you're spending too much time by yourself, but really you're just expanding your mind. Deep, man.

Typical owners: Bob Marley and Joss Stone

GREEN

You're one well-rounded person who's in tune with yourself and your surroundings. And your tunes, obviously. You've used up all the space on your iPod because you've got such varied musical taste, although you'd rather keep that whale-sounds track just between you and your iPod. You're a happy, positive kinda soul, who's not too phased by anything. And if a couple of your friends have a fight, you're always the one who steps in to get them to kiss and make up. Harmony, that's what it's all about.

Typical owners: Gwyneth Paltrow and Jake Gyllenhaal

PINK

No one's going to get an answer from your mobile on Sunday afternoon because you're always glued to the charts. You're also bang up to date with all the latest celebrity gossip and are not at all ashamed to know the name of Paris Hilton's chihuahua. But your head's not always in the clouds (or *Heat*) and you've got lots of great mates because you're kind and caring and always there with a shoulder to cry on and a headphone splitter to cheer them up with the latest tunes.

Typical owner: It has to be Pink. And Graham Norton

WHITE

Not actually a colour, more of a statement. You're an individual and would never follow trends or like a song just because everyone else does. You hate the whole *Pop Idol* thang because it's just a production line of copycat, manufactured rubbish and prefer indie bands that you're always the first to discover. But whatever your taste, you know what you like and like what you know. So you'd never be seen dead buying a cheesy compilation album and the contents of your iPod are a constant source of amazement to your friends.

Typical owners: Kelly Osbourne and David Beckham (wearing white for his club *and* country can't be a coincidence, can it?)

A DESIGN FOR LIFE

Whose hand should we shake for designing such a sleek, stunningly beautiful machine? Why, a Brit's, of course

Apple's design chief, Geordie Johnny Ives, has been nicknamed the 'David Beckham of design' after he created the iMac, iBook and G5 Power Mac. If Apple hadn't come along, Johnny's career might have gone down the lavatory – literally! He used to design toilet bowls. Not surprisingly, Johnny found the iPod a bit more inspiring. 'It could have been shaped like a banana if we'd wanted,' he says (not sure the iBanana would have caught on, though), 'because it's about listening to music, and that's what's important.' Johnny admits to having an 'obsessive attention to detail' and this can be seen everywhere on the iPod, from the serial number etched into the back (no horrible marks from sticky labels here) to the matching white power supply with retractable prongs, clam-shell packaging and that 'Enjoy' message you see when you first open the box. 'I remember there was a discussion: "Headphones can't be white – headphones are black or dark grey . . . "' Johnny put his foot down and gave us the first great icon of the twenty-first century. When you grow up and have kids, they'll be staring at it in a design museum in thirty years' time. No, really. Jolly good show, sir.

i'M a celebrity: Clothes designer Paul Smith

'I used to go everywhere with my Walkman but Jonathan Ives sent me an iPod and it's perfect. A mate put a load of stuff on it for me and I wrote down asterisks beside the ones I like - although afterwards, someone told me you can just press a button and it does it for you!'

i'M a celebrity: David Bowie

'I wished and wished and then wished again and there it was. From the wife, my iPod. Oh, happy day. I've already listed over seven hundred songs to gunge it up with.'

iSay . . .

'I love the way they look - they're beautiful bits of kit. I take mine everywhere. And I note any new scratch or smear.' William Marshall, Hong Kong

'On the bus the other day I was sitting opposite someone who had a MiniDisc and I felt really sorry for them.' Rachel Young, Nottingham

myPod

Chapter 3 >

Burn, Burn

How to cram your music on to your iPod

An iPod wouldn't be much use without any music (actually it would, see Chapter Seven - ed), so what most people do as soon as they meet their hungry new friend is quench its insatiable appetite for tunes with their own music collection. It's easiest to prepare a meal of CDs that you just feed to your computer using iTunes. It's so fast, you've barely enough time to nip to the toilet as it wolfs them down. But it's also possible to whip up a delicious concoction of miniDiscs, vinyl and even cassettes. If you've been using Musicmatch or another application and already have a digital music library, just sweep it up when prompted as you launch iTunes. Or drag and drop later. You can even continue using Musicmatch for Windows with your iPod (although iTunes must be quite good - it's the only music program ever to win a Grammy!). Silence will be golden no more . . .

ITUNES FOR CHEATS
Advanced play and tricky manoeuvres

You can find out all you ever wanted to know (and stuff you didn't) about iTunes from Apple's official site - including tips and tricks and keyboard shortcuts. But if you're one of those people who gets distracted more quickly than a three year old with ADD, here's a brief iTunes breakdown to help you become a true child of the technological revolution.

www.apple.com/support/itunes
www.apple.com/itunes/hottips

RIPPING CDs
Let's go digital!

They say that you can do anything to a CD and it will still play (although using it as a frisbee was never actually recommended), but even if you take better care of them than your pet puppy Snuffle Wuffle, they still become unreliable after fifteen years. However, if you store your music digitally on your computer, you'll have it forever and dumping your CD collection on there couldn't be easier. Just open up iTunes, insert a CD into the drive, deselect songs you don't want to transfer (like that pants a capella remix) and press import. The songs appear in your iTunes library and automatically transfer to your iPod the next time you hook up. You don't have to listen to the album as you go - turn off this option to speed up the process. Tracks are automatically converted to AAC format, but you can change this in Edit>Preferences>Importing before you insert your CD. Here you can also choose to use Error Correction, which will even allow you to import scratched CDs. If you're recording DJ mixes, classical recordings or dance music like The Avalanches, for example, that have no break between tracks, go to Advanced>Join Tracks. Or cut out that boring intro or outro by playing around with File>Get Info>Options>Start Time and Stop Time. If you want to get really fancy with editing, download some special software - MP3 TrackMaker joins or splits tracks in Windows (£8, www.heathcosoft.com) and mEdit does the job for Macs (free, www.pure-mac.com). Remember that once you've imported a CD, iTunes works a bit of magic the next time you connect to the Internet, and finds album info, like track names and artist credits from the CD Data Bank at www.gracenote.com so you don't have to spend two years typing everything in. Unless you want to. You freak.

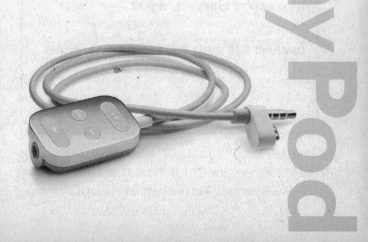

WEPOD

Cramming for an exam? Or just incredibly lazy? Get someone else to put your CDs onto your iPod

In London, the nice people at wePod will come round to your house to pick up your music collection and iPod and drop it back within five days fully loaded. Apparently it takes a whole day and night (like, twenty-four hours) of sitting in front of your computer to upload ninety album CDs, the size of an average collection. It's a godsend for people who aren't technologically minded. Law student Laura Cohen says, 'I spent two weeks downloading only five hundred songs. To this day I don't know how I managed it. Eventually I just gave up.' The wePod people also suggest giving preloaded iPods as presents. It don't come cheap, though. You'll have to part with £1 per CD for a minimum of 100 albums. But hey, you're worth it, right?

(wePod: 020 7851 0725. Similar services at www.everythingipod.co.uk)

DISPLAY

Just browsing? We're here to help

Customize the iTunes window so it displays the information you want - say, Album Title, BPM or Year Recorded - by going to Edit>View Options. Click on Browse in the top right corner of the iTunes window to get an even easier-to-manage display. To add ratings, comments, liner notes, composers' information (useful for classical music) or to alter individual volume, right-click on a song and go to Get Info. This is called 'tagging'. Like when you used to play British Bulldog at school. To change multiple tracks at the same time, highlight them first and then go to Get Info (to highlight a whole block, click on the top track and hold down Shift as you click on the bottom one or highlight at random by holding down Command (Mac) or Ctrl (Windows) as you click). Songs won't transfer to your iPod if they don't have artist and song names. If you always want certain tracks to be linked together (for example the four movements of a classical symphony), click on Edit>View Options>Grouping to see the column, then right-click on individual tracks and go to Get Info to give each one the group name. Click on the Grouping column header and your four movements won't be moving much anymore. If it bothers you that you can't see all the words in your song titles (what are you doing with 'Tie a Yellow Ribbon Round the Old Oak Tree' on there anyway?), double-click on the top of vertical column lines to fit in all the text. Move tracks into playlists by dragging and dropping or select the songs you want and then go to File>New Playlist From Selection, then give it a name. Congratulations, you have conquered Level 2. You may now move on . . .

MANUAL UPDATING
Make sure iTunes doesn't wipe your iPod

If you've got tunes from another computer on your iPod, you could lose them all when you connect back home if you're not careful. Stop your computer automatically refreshing your iPod by holding down Command/Option on the Mac or Ctrl/Shift/Alt in Windows when you hook up until its name appears in iTunes. In Manual Updating mode, it's also possible to directly remove music from your iPod by clicking on its icon in the source list, highlighting tracks and pressing Delete on the keyboard. None of this will affect iTunes until you switch back to Automatic Updating. Personally, we're waiting until some lab boffin designs some software that'll allow us to manually delete songs off the iPod when we're out and about. Or maybe it's out there somewhere, it's just that we haven't found it yet.

SOUNDCHECKING
Stop yourself looking like an idiot

When you record songs from different sources, the volume can be all over the place. If you see someone wearing white headphones suddenly jump a metre in the air as they desperately scrabble to take their earbuds out, it's because they haven't been using Soundcheck and the next song's come on about five times louder than the last. Prevent embarrassing Decibel Shock situations by turning on Soundcheck in iTunes in Preferences>Effects to set all tracks to the same volume level. Remember that you then need to activate Soundcheck on your iPod, too. Otherwise all your hard work will have been for nothing. Fool.

EQUALIZING
Fine-tune your settings to your surroundings

Ever got on the bus while listening to your iPod and found that you suddenly can't hear any bass? Here's how to custom-make EQ presets so you can tweak your iPod's settings at the touch of a button. You can only use one home-made EQ preset at a time on the iPod, so decide when you're most likely to use it, say to play through your home stereo. Click on the Equalizer button in the bottom right corner of the iTunes window. Then either adapt one of the standard EQ presets or go to Manual and create your own. Pump up the bass for playing through small speakers. Use the Classical EQ preset for when you're jetting off on holiday to boost high and low frequencies, which helps in very noisy environments, or boost the treble to play through your hi-fi if your front room's full of sound-absorbent sofas, curtains and furnishings.

Once you've done the DIY, click on Make Preset and give it a name, say Public Transport, Travel Speakers or Drown Out Dad's Pink Floyd albums. Set up a playlist in iTunes and assign all tracks the preset. Transfer to your iPod and everything will play as normal. But when you get on that bus, just go to Settings>EQ and choose any setting to activate (iTunes overrides the iPod). Magic.

VISUALS

You can still get cool artwork with your music, you know. And more . . .

Songs you download from the iTunes Music Store often come with their own artwork, just like buying a CD from the high street. If not, download official album graphics from www.allmusic.com or www.amazon.co.uk. Or sit back and put your feet up while a couple of nifty pieces of add-on freeware do it for you — download Clutter for Macs (http://sprote.com/clutter) or iArt 1.0 for Windows (www.ipodlounge.com). If you're doing it manually, just highlight a track, click on the Show Song Artwork button below the Source list and just drag and drop graphics into the small window that appears.

You can add any JPEG, TIFF, GIF, PNG, Photoshop file, your own digital photos and even the first page of a PDF document. To attach one image to multiple tracks, highlight them all before you drag and drop. Click on images to make them full screen and right-click to delete.

Want to watch old-skool rave graphics as you play your music? Turn on Visuals by clicking on the flower icon in the bottom right of the iTunes window (press '?' to change waveforms and colours).

Download freeware to get more exciting screensavers - try sites like Version Tracker (www.versiontracker.com) or programs such as WhiteCap (www.55ware.com/whitecapdownload.html) or EasyView for Mac (www.trinfinitysoftware.com/easyview.shtml), which combines track info into the visuals as part of that whole multimedia experience.

LISTENING TO THE RADIO
Ooh, how old-fashioned!

It's very easy to dial up Internet radio in iTunes, although you need to adjust the bit-stream rate depending on the speed of your connection. If the reception's jumpier than a kangaroo on a pogo stick, this'll be why. You can't listen to a station that has a higher bit-stream rate than your modem so, for example, because 56Kbps (kilo bits per second) modems actually connect at a slightly slower speed, change your radio setting to 32Kbps. If you're still having problems, go to Edit>Preferences>Advanced>Streaming Buffer Size and choose Large. You can listen to local radio or Outer Mongolian FM (great for practising your language skills!), as long as it broadcasts in MP3 - type in the web address or go to www.shoutcast.com for a comprehensive list of stations. Now you're on the right wavelength.

ENCODING

You're a sucker for punishment, aren't you?

Within each format, be it AAC, MP3 or whatever, it's possible to change individual file quality, like increasing pixels in a digital photograph to get a sharper picture. The default setting for AAC files in iTunes is 128Kbps, the CD standard. The encoding options can be viewed in Edit>Preferences>Importing. If you're importing MP3s, which are slightly inferior to AAC, you could choose the High Quality option (160Kbps) or Higher Quality (192Kbps). On the other hand, if you are short of space on your hard disk, you could import AAC files as 96Kbps (near CD Quality) and MP3s as Good Quality (128Kbps), while voice recordings come out fine in 64Kbps (FM Radio Quality). Save even more space by choosing Joint Stereo under Stereo Mode as it eliminates sounds that are identical in both ears. With voice recordings and sound effects, import them as Mono rather than Stereo under Channels.

There's also Variable Bit Rate (VBR) encoding, which comes into its own for classical music as it makes sure that you can hear everything in complicated passages where the whole orchestra is belting out, and then economizes during the quieter oboe solo as you don't need the full range of sound. This could take up either less or more space on the hard drive, depending on the piece. However, most people leave encoding well alone and never notice the difference. Aah, ignorance is bliss.

MAC V WINDOWS
How to switch between operating systems

If you use both regularly, say at home and at work or school, format your iPod in Windows and the Mac will sync perfectly with it too, doubling the fun. Just remember to always have Manual Updating switched on in iTunes or you'll replace all the iPod's songs when you connect. If you need to swap from Mac to Windows, restore it (losing all the data on your iPod) using the software updater on your CD or from the Apple website.

SMART PLAYLISTS
Imagine you're Marilyn Manson's PA and he'll only listen to songs with the word 'blood' in them. Your life just got a whole lot easier.

This is how you can listen to your music in completely new ways. Set up smart playlists by going to File>New Smart Playlist and clicking on the + button to add multiple conditions. Switch on Live Updating to keep it up to date. If you tag tracks in the Comments fields (through Get Info), iTunes gives you unlimited possibilities. Create a Monday Morning Playlist to get you revved up for the week (BPM>140), a Christmas playlist so you don't have to listen to your parents' dusty old Bing Crosby records (Song Name contains 'Christmas'+Year Recorded>1995), or even an Absent Friends Playlist to remind you of your best pal, Alex (Comment is Alex's fave). If you're stuck for ideas, check out seriously spoddy site www.smartplaylists.com, where users describe how they created theirs. Don't lose sleep over storage space if you've put your favourite Busted track in twenty-eight different playlists. It's not clogging up your hard disk as playlists are just shortcuts to your library. Whether it's clogging up your brain is a different matter entirely.

The Visiting Relatives Playlist

(Song Title contains 'Family', 'Bored', 'Argue', 'Mother' + artist contains 'Family')

'Can't Stand Your Mother' - *Lucy Pearl*

'Bored Out Of My Mind'

- *Manic Street Preachers*

'No Need To Argue' - *The Cranberries*

'Cretin Family' - *The Ramones*

'Run' - *Lighthouse Family*

The Tidying Bedroom Playlist

(Song Title contains 'Clean', 'Bed' + 'Hang')

'Cleaning Out My Closet' - *Eminem*

'Bedroom Bounty Hunter' - *Shaggy*

'So Fresh So Clean' - *Outkast*

'Jacket Hangs' - *The Blue Aeroplanes*

'Bed I Never Made' - *Lamya*

The Relationship's Over Playlist

(Last Played is 'Last Time You Split Up With Someone')

'You Make Me Sick' - *Pink*

'Get Out Of My House' - *The Streets*

'Caught Out There (I Hate You So Much Right Now)' - *Kelis*

'Lost Without You' - *Delta Goodrem*

'Hello, I Love You Won't You Tell Me Your Name' - The Doors

RECORDING FROM MINIDISC, VINYL AND CASSETTES

The ease depends on your computer. But even if you've got a ten-year-old PC that's bigger than your fridge, it can be done.

HARDWARE: If you have a newer Mac with built-in mic or a Windows PC with external soundcard, sit back and put your feet up. All you need is a cable with two red and black inputs to connect to the Line Out on your stereo and a 3.5mm jack on the other end to plug into your computer. All electrical shops sell them and you can use the same cable to play your iPod through the home stereo. If you're recording from vinyl, run your decks through an amp or mixer to boost the volume and connect the cable to that. It's possible to record through the Mic In or Line In port, but you'll need to turn the source volume right down in Control Panels to reduce distortion, and even then it's unlikely you'll get a clean take. You'll get much better stereo quality (in and out) by using an external audio interface connected to your USB port such as the Griffin iMic (£31.95, www.everythingipod.co.uk) or PowerWave (£100, www.griffintechnology.com/products) that comes with Final Vinyl software for audio editing. You can now record from your stereo, plug in a microphone to dictate your deepest thoughts or connect to your amp to capture those rockin' guitar solos. If you've got Apple's Garageband music sequencer, you can even create your own songs and dance tracks for loading up to your iPod so you can go off and wow record company execs.

SOFTWARE: You've got music flowing into your computer - now you need to record it. The good news is that you can get the software for free. Yay! On new Macs, record audio through iMovie or Sound Studio while PCs also come with bundled recording and editing software. If you have an older machine, find shareware at www.hitsquad.com/smm/cat/AUDIO_RECORDING such as Amadeus II, Audiocorder, BIAS Peak, Final Vinyl and Sound Studio for Mac, and Audio Editor/Recorder, GoldWave and RIP Vinyl for Windows. PC users can also use Audacity (http://audacity.sourceforge.net/) or Musicmatch, the software that used to come with your iPod before iTunes For Windows (www.musicmatch.com). If you're recording a lot of vinyl, get rid of scratches and crackles with some of the audio editors mentioned above or download freeware like DePopper 1.01 or WaveLab (www.download.com or www.hitsquad.com).

But before you start recording all seventy-four minutes of Beethoven's Ninth Symphony, test out the levels. Go to Sound in The Control Panel and change the input source and then adjust the volume against the loudest part of your song (play around with the volume on your stereo too). It'll take some experimenting before you get the right balance. Depending on the software, you might improve sound quality by saving files as AIFF or WAV but make sure that you've got enough room on your hard disk - one hour's music takes up 600MB of storage space. Compress the files later by converting to either MP3 or AAC in iTunes.

i'M a celebrity: Kevin Bacon

'I use my iPod to record music that I write. I create a lot on film sets, where I set up a mini-studio in my trailer. I find it the most relaxing way to spend my downtime.'

BURNING CDs

You're not going to give them to your friends, though, are you? Cos that would be, like, illegal

Once your music's on the computer, it's a piece of cake to transfer it to your iPod or burn CDs to play at other people's houses. You'll need a blank recordable disk (CD-R) from any electrical shop, which plays for seventy-four to eighty minutes. First, construct a playlist in iTunes and change each track's format to AIFF or WAV. You can't change the format of AAC files purchased from iTunes Music Store (although you can burn them as they are) and you can't burn Audible book files. Check how much space in minutes your playlist is going to take up at the bottom of the iTunes browser and allow an extra minute for breaks between songs. Open up Edit>Preferences>Burning to set the size of the gap between tracks and click on

Soundcheck (assuming you're already using it in iTunes) so that each song will play at the same volume. Also check that the Preferred Speed is the same as that written on your CD-R. It's worth taking your time to make sure everything's hunky-dory because if you make a hash of it, you can't start again and will just have to use a new blank disc. Now select your playlist, insert the CD-R and click on Burn Disc in the top right of the iTunes window. This is the only time in life when seeing a radioactive symbol is good news — the operation was successful, Mr Bond, ha-ha-ha-ha-ha.

Don't use other applications, the keyboard or the mouse, and make sure your computer doesn't go to sleep or use a screensaver while burning or you could cause it to jump. When it's finished, add all the song info by going to File>Export Song List and saving as a text file. If you're a real flash Harry and have a CD/MP3 player, you can also burn songs in MP3 format. CD-Rs take 650MB of data (check how many megabytes your playlist is at the bottom of the iTunes browser), which means you can get up to twelve hours' play on just one CD! Whatever will they think of next? Oh . . . iPods, of course.

BACKING UP

Yawn . . .

Yes, it's boring, way too sensible and the kind of thing your dad might do, but you'll be so glad you backed up if your PC goes belly-up. Transfer your entire digital music library by saving it on an MP3 CD or, if you have the right drive, a data CD or DVD (a single DVD can house 4.7GB or 150 CDs!). Make up a playlist to back up and keep an eye on the amount of megabytes at the bottom of the iTunes browser to make sure it'll fit. As you're probably constantly refining your iTunes library, remember what you've backed up already by creating a Smart Playlist with Live Updating activated that includes everything you've added since your last bout of spoddiness.

PLAYING THROUGH YOUR STEREO

Cos music was meant to be shared, right?

Connecting your iPod up to your home speakers couldn't be easier. All you need is a 3.5mm jack to red-and-black stereo input cable from your local electrical shop (the same cable you use between your stereo and computer) to plug into Aux In, Tape In or CD In on the hi-fi. Set the iPod volume to just under half and control the output through your stereo. Now the whole house can hear that fab limited-edition white label.

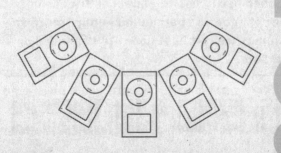

PROTECTION
The iPod's dangerously cool

With a continuous stream of tunes in your pocket and those new sound-enhancing headphones, it's easy to walk around like a zombie from *Shaun Of The Dead*. Which is not a good idea in heavy traffic or on a canal towpath. And while the iPod's a handy tool for avoiding hassle from charity muggers and mad people on buses, if you can't hear the nice assistant shout, 'Next!' in the queue at Starbucks you might be in for a few verbals from the people behind you. Slightly more worrying is that those trademark white headphones could turn you into a sitting duck for muggers. Gary Parkinson of *Stuff* magazine, says, 'The iPod is so shiny and lovely you always want to get it out and show people. But this attracts criminals like magpies. People should use the remote and keep the iPod in a pocket.' Either that or get a different set of headphones (see chapter eight).

But the most important thing to remember is not to endanger friendships, so if you're borrowing your mate's, always treat it as if your life depended on it. Safe.

i'M a celebrity: Peaches Geldof

'I'd love an iPod but my computer is basically from the 70s, so I can't download songs. I act nonchalant if anyone asks me to listen to theirs, but secretly I'm really envious. If I had one, it'd have a lot of rock music on it - The Stones, The Kinks, The Strokes . . .'

iSay . . .

'I listen to my iPod as I go to sleep, but sometimes I don't want to take it off. I say to myself one more song and find myself awake at five o'clock in the morning.' Anon

'I used to take an extra backpack when I travelled just for my CDs. Now I just bring my iPod. And I can put photos and files on it too.' Stephen Gundee, Colorado, US

'The beautiful design makes it so appealing, but the best thing is its size. I imported all my six-hundred CDs and now they're all in boxes under my bed.' Nick Dastoor, Glasgow

'With Shuffle, sometimes I can sense what's coming up. My iPod knows me and knows what I'm doing. The other day I was walking into a churchyard and it started playing Jeff Buckley's "Hallelujah" - it was an amazing moment.' Hannah, London

Chapter 4 >

I Fought the Law...

. . . and the law won. How downloading music from the Internet became a crime

The record companies got themselves in a right old tizz about downloading music. They said that CD sales were down thirty per cent because of illegal Internet file-sharing and started accusing anyone who'd ever even heard of the old Napster (which they eventually got closed down) of stealing music. Boardroom types claimed that ninety per cent of people downloading music were doing it illegally.

First they tried to sue peer-to-peer (P2P) websites like KaZaA, that supply the software for finding and downloading music from other people's computers, and when that failed they got personal and went after little old us, by getting our names from ISPs. In the US, four students using high-speed college computers to make thousands of songs available on campus networks had to pay up to £10,000 each. Over 2,000 lawsuits were launched as record companies also used the courts to demand money from home users, like a twelve-year-old schoolgirl from Manhattan and a seventy-one-year-old granddad from Texas - people who didn't even realize that others could access their computers to share their music.

But this frightening scenario isn't just limited to the States — 250 cases have already been brought against users in Canada, Denmark, Germany and Italy by European bodies who say that they are breaking copyright law. They claim to be only targeting 'major offenders' who have over 1,000 songs on their hard disk but for anyone who's got an iPod, that's only enough tracks to fill a mini! The more files you have, the more steam comes out of their ears.

In the UK, the British Phonographic Industry says it's ready to sue Music fans who use illegal sites and they will target users by sending instant warning messages to individual PCs. A big job - they've got any one of an estimated 7.4 million (that's one in eight) people to choose from.

Last year's European copyright law made downloading certain files a criminal offence - even if they're just for your own use - and you can be fined or cop two years in the slammer (surely it's Peter Andre who should be locked up for 'Insania', not us for copying it?). But don't start tying bricks to your computer and dumping it in the North Sea just yet. In America, record companies offered an amnesty (i.e., they'd let you off) if people put their hands up and admitted they were guilty, erased illegal files and signed an agreement promising not to do it again, very sorry, sir. It should happen in the UK too.

The scare tactics are working. The number of shared music files on KaZaA dropped from 900 to 550 million. But many people believe that illegal file-sharing actually encourages us to buy *more* CDs because we have access to a greater range of music. They argue that if you never hear a song, you'll never know if you like it. A study by boffins at America's Harvard Business School and the University of North Carolina found that for the most popular albums, every 150 free downloads increased sales by one copy. What do the record companies make of this, we wonder?

POP STARS

How Pepsi shook up the business

In February 2004, Pepsi announced it was giving away 100 million free downloads from the iTunes Music Store in an ad shown during the

American equivalent of the FA Cup Final, the Superbowl. Pepsi used sixteen American teenagers who had been sued for illegally downloading music from P2P sites. In the advert, fourteen-year-old New Yorker Annie Leith says, 'Hi, I'm one of the kids who was prosecuted for downloading music. And I'm here to announce in front of 100 million people that we're still going to download music free off the Internet.' Through Pepsi's giveaway, of course. Annie's family had been forced to shell out £1,700 after Annie, her older sister and younger brother downloaded nearly 1,000 songs from KaZaA. But at least she could use some of her Pepsi fee to pay her parents back.

Michelle Maalouf, a thirteen-year-old from San Francisco, was another of the teens in the ad. Along with her seventeen-year-old sister, Kristina, she was done for downloading songs by Pink, Norah Jones and Ja Rule. 'I didn't think it was that big a deal,' says Kristina. 'Everybody I know was downloading music.' They didn't even realize they were sharing files with other KaZaA users or how to turn the function off. 'It was fun being in the commercial, but being sued wasn't so great,' adds Michelle. 'We didn't know it was illegal. We weren't ripping off the artists - we still bought CDs and went to concerts.' And when it came out that the Maaloufs had made a CD of downloaded tunes for a school assignment, lawyers even wanted them to reveal the names of their classmates and teacher. They refused to grass and were hit with an even bigger fine.

The record companies lost even more friends when they went after seventy-one-year-old Durwood Pickle, whose grandchildren had downloaded music on his computer when they'd visited, and twelve-year-old Brianna LaHara, whose mum had to stump up £1,100. 'I got really scared. My stomach was all turning,' said Brianna. 'I thought it was OK to download music because my mum paid a fee. Out of all people, why did they pick me? I don't want to hurt the artists I love.'

And complete pandemonium broke out in the corridors of Princeton Uni, New Jersey, after a lawsuit was brought against Daniel Peng, who had set up a search engine for downloadable songs and movies. He could have been fined £82,000 per track. 'His life was thrown into chaos,' says friend Powell Fraser. It put The Fear into plenty of other students too. 'Some sprinted back to their rooms to wipe their hard disks clean,' adds Powell. In the end, Daniel was forced to cough up £12,500 (the equivalent of ninety-two minis!) and the seventeen-year-old replaced his search engine with a web page asking for donations. By June 2004, he'd raised nearly half.

iSay . . .

'I admit I use illegal sites to download music. But if it's good, I'll go out and buy it ninety per cent of the time because if some band "touches" me, I want to repay them and I also like the cover art. Downloading music isn't killing the industry - it's changing it, giving it a new lease of life.' Anon

It's a fair cop, guv

Hello, hello, hello, what do we have here, then? It's not just those white earphones that give you away. Here are ten other signs that you're an iPod owner:

Bruises on your forehead
From walking into walls while changing playlists

Highly developed thumb muscles
Scroll! Scroll! Scroll!

You know the date of Steve Jobs's birthday
And you send him a card every year

Bags under your eyes
From sleep deprivation trying to beat the Solitaire world record

You've taken up jogging
Just so you could buy one of those snazzy iPod armbands

You've changed your Internet homepage
It's now the iPodlounge, natch

There are no CDs in your bedroom
Cos you've ripped them all and sold them on ebay

You've put on a few pounds
Big Macs with free iTunes downloads? It's the ultimate double whammy

You think you've got tinnitus
Because you never take those earphones out

You're handcuffed
Been illegal downloading again, have we, sir?

THE GREY ALBUM

What's illegal and what isn't?

Downloading music from the Internet can seem like crossing a minefield. But remember that what's important is not which website you're using but how you use it. Sharing copy-protected files is illegal. So think of your digital music files in the same way as a CD collection – you wouldn't share yours with complete strangers, would you? Or go round their house and help yourself? So if you're downloading a song for free that you know you'd have to pay top dollar for in a music shop down the high street, most likely you're breaking the law. Basically, if something looks too good to be true, it probably is. You could land yourself in trouble for file-sharing copy-protected music on KaZaA, Grokster, Gnutella, Morpheus, Soulseek, Freenet, LimeWire, DirectConnect and iMesh among others.

Even more confusingly, using sites with non-copyright files that claim to be kosher could land you in hot water too. For example, Spanish-based WebListen gives money to songwriters, and for £23 a month you can download unlimited MP3s and WMAs from its 140,000-track library. And the Russian AllofMP3 charges just £9 for 1,000 MP3 files per month - that's 30p an album in any format - and pays fees to local copyright holders. But legal types say these sites are not giving a share to the artist, record label *and* producers and you would therefore be breaking the law for subscribing.

Even if you've legally bought that new Fatboy Slim remix, you could be done up like a kipper for putting it on a mix CD for your best mate. Yes, really. As your mate hasn't paid any copyright fees, it's just another way of sharing your music files illegally, you see. So where *can* you find music that won't have you hiding behind the sofa with every ring of the doorbell? Read on . . .

STILL BORED?

Ten thousand songs not enough for you? Here're five cool websites to keep you amused.

Work out your height in iPods.
This automatic converter is like a modern-day version of measuring horses with hands. It only works with white iPods so if you've got a mini, you're going to have to do it yourself. Well, you did say you were bored . . . (www.ipodhead.com)

Own up to the worst song on your iPod.
C'mon, don't be shy - Sisqo's Thong Song is in the all-time Top Ten. Surely yours can't be any worse. Can it? (www.ipodlaughs.com)

Review the iPod's extensive film and music career.
The little fella will soon be commanding multimillion-dollar appearance fees after starring in movies *Runaway Jury*, *Agent Cody Banks* and *The Italian Job*; TV shows *The O.C.*, *Alias*, *The Sopranos* and *ER* and music vids such as 50 Cent's 'Pimp', Mary J Blige's 'Love At First Sight' and Obie Trice's 'Got Sum Teef'. Enough to give J.Lo a run for her money (www.ipodlounge.com/forums). Or check out iPocalypse Photoshop, where the iPod's been inserted into movie stills to boost its career prospects even further. Write your own captions or laugh at other

people's lame attempts at humour. (www.ipodlaughs.com)

Have a look inside your iPod without taking it apart.
It's all very well dissecting frogs in biology lessons (no, it's not - ed) but you wouldn't want to cut up your iPod. Fortunately, someone else has done it for you (see Pictures Of Ipod In Pieces at www.ipod-ing.com).

Read people's rejected iPod engravings. Although personally we can't see anything wrong with 'Weapons of mass distraction inside' or 'Your mamma uses a Walkman' (www.methodshop.com).

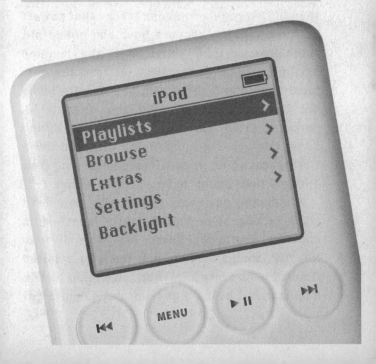

myPod

Chapter 5 >

Surfin' UK

Blighty goes downloading crazy

Internet music shopping kicked off like the January sales with the arrival of broadband. Suddenly you could download a track in about a minute, around - gasp - twenty times faster than with a regular modem. Tracks that cut off halfway through because your dog pulled out the wires or your sister used the landline became a thing of the past. At first the only legal sites were in the USA, and despite being on the 'worldwide' web you needed an American credit card to use them. But, during 2004, cartoon-style lightbulbs flickered on in the heads of UK record companies and they allowed their songs to be released online.

We finally got some high-profile download sites of our own. MyCokeMusic launched in January, and soon there was the all-new Napster, Sony's Connect and the long-awaited iTunes Music Store (iTMS) UK. Sure, you had to pay now, but at least you weren't going to get fined ten years' pocket money or, more likely, download some nasty virus, spyware or impossible-to-shake pop-up ads sneakily hiding in that Mis-Teeq single.

People who were used to secret file-sharing came out of the closet and went straight. Even if you've never used a P2P site (honest, officer) they did us *all* a favour by forcing down prices. So not only are CDs now way cheaper, but online tracks are just 80-99p - good value for a quality file that's easy to find, can be safely downloaded in the time it takes you to make a brew and is available on 'radio date'. Plus you can go shopping for that Scissor Sisters album at three in the morning if you feel like it. The doors are always open. And once you've bought it you're not going to leave it on the bus or forget which friend you lent it to.

Most sites now also sell tracks you can't find on the high street - and not just any old whack either. The Thrills released a live five-track session on iTMS forty-eight hours after recording it at a Californian radio station and the site also features around 150 exclusives at any one time. The Rolling Stones gathered no moss by putting 500 songs from their back catalogue online and George Michael has said he'll release all his new music on his website for free: instead of helping to pay for another fat-cat music mogul's Rolls-Royce, fans can make a donation to charity.

Not surprisingly, in February 2004 downloads overtook record-shop single sales in the UK for the first time. New sites from big playas are turning up on Google all the time - by the time you read this, Yahoo, AOL, MTV, Real, Musicmatch, Amazon and, er, Tesco could all be selling us music online. In a few years, a band might get to No 1 on *Top Of The Pops* without anyone having bought their single in a record shop like HMV or Virgin and they'll have to change the name of *CD:UK* to *Download: UK*. So long as it's still presented by Cat Deeley . . .

MIND YOUR MP3s AND FAQs
Check you're on top format

As we've told you a gadzillion times already, the iPod isn't like other digital music players. And don't you go forgetting, otherwise you'll download a bunch of tunes that won't even allow you to look at the artwork, let alone play. While you'll no doubt be spending many an afternoon browsing the aisles of iTMS, if you get tempted by a fancy window display and pop into a rival store, always check the small print before you buy.

Most official downloads are protected with something called DRM, which is a piece of computer code attached to your music that has instructions on how it can be used - to prevent copying or trading on P2P sites. Firstly, don't worry about straight MP3s as they're never coded and always up for a spin on your iPod. Obviously you can also play AAC files from iTMS. But the commonly used WMA format is a whole different kettle of fish. If the file's copy-protected with DRM, you can forget about it. If not, you can play it on your iPod if you put in a bit of mousework. First burn it to a CD and, as you do, convert it to AAC or MP3 in the Edit>Preferences>Importing menu. Then just eject the disc and reinsert it to upload into iTunes, and you're good to go (although converting a compressed format to another loses data so you end up with a lower quality recording).

However, since Apple's link-up with Windows-based HP computers, the word on the street is that iPods will be enabled to play all WMAs directly in the future, so you'll be able to download from the sites in this chapter without restriction. For now, you can use sites like Napster 2.0 and KaZaA as a huge reference library - they all allow you to hear thirty-second previews or stream tracks for free (you might have to download Windows Music Player). Then check out the search engine MP3.com (www.mp3.com) to find out where to locate tracks in the format you want (it has free thirty-second streams too) or go to www.amazon.co.uk and buy the track on CD for a similar price (and a higher quality file). You might have to wait a couple more days, but we're assuming your mental age is over three and you've stopped saying things like, 'But I want it NOW!' Plus, you still don't have to leave the house. You should go out sometimes, though. Even if it's just to take your iPod for a walk.

Steve Jobs was the first guy to persuade major record labels to make their music available all on one website. He also met with twenty top artists, including Bono, Moby, Mick Jagger and Sheryl Crow to ensure that all the big boys were on board. 'We've shown there's a way out of this mess - that there's a legal alternative that's better than stealing,' he said. 'iTunes has revolutionized the way people buy music online.' He wasn't just talking it up. By far the largest and most popular music download site, customers were buying 2.7 million songs a week in the US when Apple released iTMS UK. Boasting 700,000 tracks, exclusives from the likes of the Beastie Boys and Alanis Morissette and retro classics such as out-of-print 60s Motown singles (as well as 5,000 audio books), iTMS is a musical education. There are biographies and interviews, if-you-like-that-you'll-love-this links and celebrity and fellow users' playlists (iMix) to take you off on completely unexpected musical tangents. So, if you like The Libertines, say, you might come across another fan's playlist and suddenly discover this 'new band' called The Clash. Plus there's a free thirty-second preview so you can try before you buy (if you've got a slow connection, click on Edit>Preferences>Store>Load A Complete Song Before Playing to prevent jumps). No more buying albums because you believed the hype, then having to take them back to CDs'R'Us the following week.

Other features: Just Added link for latest tunes, music videos to watch while browsing, movie trailers, official CD inserts for printing and gift certificates. So now you know what to get all your iPod buddies for Christmas.

Cost: 79p per track

Format: AAC (DRM)

www.apple.com/uk/itunes

i'M a celebrity: Alicia Keys

'*I'm the type of artist who wants to reach a lot of people, and the iTunes Music Store is the best way in the world to do that.*'

NAPSTER 2.0

Once the sworn enemy of the record industry, Napster has now gone legit. Launched in 1999 by nineteen-year-old Shawn Fanning from his uncle's garage, at its peak it had an incredible 100 million users but was forced to shut up shop after a long series of legal battles. But Roxio bought the name and hired Shawn as a consultant - so Napster 2.0 has kept its chatty style, community spirit and best features like online magazine *Fuzz*, interactive radio stations, plus email and chat rooms. It's no longer a P2P site, but with over 750,000 songs in the library, we're not complaining.

Other features: Watch music videos, browse the UK charts from 1994 and check out what other people are listening to/view their libraries (though you can't nick stuff any more!).

Cost: The £9.95 a month subscription (with free seven-day trial) allows you to download or stream as many tracks as you like, but you have to pay 99p each to burn. Free thirty-second previews.

Format: WMA (DRM)

www.napster.co.uk

MYCOKEMUSIC.COM

It beat iTMS and Napster into Europe but it's not as huge and doesn't have the same cool factor. But it does great giveaways (20 million free downloads was The Real Thing), there are three exclusives a week and as Coca-Cola sponsors the charts, there's a hell of a lot of pop. As you'd expect from a fizzy drinks company. The 300,000 tracks are broken down into genres - nice to see Deutsch Pop and German Schlager lovers catered for, for once! One advantage over iTMS is that if you buy a song and then lose it down the back of your computer, you can just go back and download it again. For nowt.

Cost: From 99p per track (discounts available). Free thirty-second previews or stream whole songs for 1p! Which ain't bad - even penny sweets cost tuppence these days.

Format: WMA (DRM)

www.mycokemusic.com

Similar sites: HMV Downloads (www.hmv.co.uk), Ministry Of Sound (www.ministryof

sound.com/home), MSN Music Club (www.msn.co.uk), Oxfam (www.bignoise music.com, where 10% goes to charity so you can clear your conscience of all that illegal downloading), Tiscali (www.tiscali.co.uk), Virgin (www.virginmegastores.co.uk) and Wanadoo Music Club (www.wana doo.co.uk/music)

KaZaA

The P2P site now sells high-quality legal downloads straight from the record companies' mouths - find files marked with a Gold Icon and you've, er, struck gold. Most are copy protected but you can listen to a sample or trial for free. You can also find legal computer games, music videos and ringtones and free music by new bands. Stay on the right side of the law by adjusting the sharing option to prevent other users accessing your copy-protected music. KaZaA's best feature is its interactiveness - users recommend tracks by email and SMS or share playlists. And if you miss the whole package of buying a CD with liner notes and artwork, how about KaZaA Kapsules? Your music download comes with lyrics, digital photos and video clips of live gigs.

Cost: Trial songs for free for a limited period and then price varies per track.

Format: Gold Files vary, but all have DRM. www.kazaa.com

WIPPIT

It's a file-sharing site, but you wouldn't know it as only 'approved' songs can be swapped. Wippit has signed a deal with 200 record labels, including heavyweights EMI and BMG, and has 60,000 tracks on its UK-based site. As well as music there are audio books, interviews with bands such as Linkin Park, Missy Elliott and Destiny's Child, stand-up comedy from Rowan Atkinson, Eddie Izzard, Steve Coogan and Harry Enfield, computer games and ringtones and even 3,000 pieces of classical music. Which is probably more than you'll want to listen to in your lifetime. And, despite having a massive music library split into over seventy genres, it's extremely easy to use, cheap and does everything you could possibly want.

Cost: Popular singles 99p or subscribe for unlimited downloads for £50 a year or £12.99 a month. No free samples, though.

Format: MP3, WMA (DRM)

www.wippit.com

PLAYLOUDER

Billed as a UK 'music service provider' - in other words, Playlouder supplies broadband for a similar price to BT or AOL (£25ish), but part of your sub goes to artists and record companies so you can share proper, licensed files with fellow subscribers in a 'gated community'. Like if you lived in a Beverly Hills mansion with Rottweilers on the door and private security firms, you could still pop over the fence to your neighbour's and use the swimming pool. If you already have an ISP, check out the download shop anyway - it's Nirvana for indie music fans. Labels Ninja Tunes, Beggars Groups, XL Recordings and V2 Music are all signed up - find tracks by White Stripes, Dizzee Rascal, The Pixies, Throwing Muses, etc. Playlouder's an off-the-wall, proud-to-be-British, mag-style site with news, reviews, features, gig guides, competitions, prizes and chat rooms. Turn it up!

Cost: 99p per track, £2 per EP or £9.99 per album - stream tracks for free. Also three free MP3s a month from up-and-coming bands.

Format: MP3, WMA (DRM)

www.playlouder.com

INDEPENDENT RECORD LABELS

If you're an indie fan, check out Matador Records (www.matadorrecords.com/mp3), which has free MP3 tasters from Dizzee Rascal and Pretty Girls Make Graves et al, while Subpop (www.subpop.com) dangles carrots in the shape of Mudhoney and The Shins. If you're more of an Ibiza kinda person, check out Trax2Burn (www.trax2burn.com) where you can download 99p MP3s from house music legends Armand Van Helden, Fatboy Slim and A Man Called Adam. Featuring dance labels End Recordings, Underwater, Shaboom, Southern Fried and more, this is the place to come if Apple ever puts mixing software on the iPod. Keep your hands in the air for London dance label Warp Records (www.bleep.com), where you can buy MP3s for 99p a shout and Deep Rhythms (www.deep-rhythms.com), which has free deep house MP3s from Finnish DJ Timo Rotonen. C'mon!

UNDERGROUND AND UNSIGNED ARTISTS

Broaden your musical horizons, man, at US site Epitonic (www.epitonic.com), which has free streams and MP3s from less well-known artists. One or two tracks from an album are available - record label bods hope that you'll then go out and buy the CD. Great for cross-referencing - especially through Epitonic Radio, which selects similar tracks to the one you started with. Or check out Vitaminic (www.vitaminic.co.uk), a European site with free MP3s from 20,000 artists hoping to get a record contract. Just imagine if they all did - you wouldn't be able to walk down the street without getting hit by a flying telly. Mperia does the same in the States (www.mperia.com). It charges around 50p per track - seventy per cent goes to the artist. So, if you buy one, they might be able to afford some milk to put on their Cheerios. Or check out any of the clutch of websites spawned by Apple's music sequencer Garageband, where users can upload tracks they've made in their bedrooms. If you fancy yourself as the next Simon Fuller (you know, the guy that discovered the Spice Girls), browse these sites, downloading free MP3s, until you find your own Daniel Bedingfield. This time next year, you'll be a millionaire. (www.macband.com, www.macidol.com, www.macjams.com, http://macjukebox.net, www.tuneyard.com)

WEIRD STUFF

Free Solo Piano (www.freesolopiano.com) has . . . OK, you can probably work this one out for yourselves. Great for fans of Yanni and Barry Manilow. Or inspiration for Grade 5 students everywhere. Just ten minutes more practice each night and one day . . . just maybe . . . you could be giving your piano recitals away for free on this site. Also check out TV Cream (www.tv.cream.org) that has loads of free MP3s of theme tunes of TV shows from the 60s to 80s that you'll recognize from Saturday afternoon repeats. Not content with just the clip used for telly, they've uploaded whole songs, as well as bizarre and hilarious cover versions. Tell your dad about it - he'll up your allowance straight away. And if you ever get stressed out, escape from it all with Quiet American (www.quietamerican.org), where you can pretend you're on a round-the-world trip with this free MP3 collection of everyday sounds from Southeast Asia - crickets, markets, local musicians, monks and drunken tourists all feature. Let your iPod transport you to a place far, far away. Like a magic carpet. Aaaaaaaaah.

SONGS IN THE KEY OF LIFE

Where to listen to your iPod

Brick In The Wall: Pink Floyd.
Outside the school gates. Cos it contains the immortal line: 'Oi, teacher, leave those kids alone.'

Superstar: Jamelia.
As you're scoring a goal for the school footy team. Although the games teacher might freak out.

Crashed The Wedding: Busted.
During the 'disco' at your auntie's third marriage.

A Grand Don't Come For Free: The Streets.
When your parents refuse to give you your allowance because you were listening to your iPod at said wedding.

21 Questions: 50 Cent.
When you get arrested for downloading music illegally.

i'M a celebrity: Alanis Morissette

'Recently I've been downloading a lot of Eminem. He's a talented guy. But my most-listened-to artist changes all the time.'

i'M a celebrity: Joaquin Phoenix

'I have my entire music collection in my iPod and take it with me when I travel. It's changed my life, because carrying my CDs around was a pain. I found myself buying the same ones all the time. I have duplicates of every Beatles album.'

iSay . . .

'I'm obsessed with my iPod. It's like having a personal soundtrack to your life that fits in your back pocket.' Megan McAllen, New Jersey, USA

'I listen to my iPod when I'm commuting - it gives my journey a soundtrack. I don't spend time making compilations any more. It's like having a brand new tape every day.' Dave Rice, Brighton

myPod

Chapter 6 >

Together in Electric Dreams

Don't keep it to yourself - the iPod's more of a people magnet than a cute puppy

When 'responsible' adults blather on about how it's not good for you to wander around all day wearing headphones, not talking to your friends or playing 'catch' or 'tag' or whatever else it was they used to do for laughs, you can tell them that just by owning an iPod puts you in a very special members-only club. One where you can make new friends just by spotting someone else with white earphones. A secret society where you get The Nod Of Respect from complete strangers. Like-minded souls who'll let you plug your earphones into their iPod for a minute or so to experience their own personal world, new mates who you can share your music with through split headphones or special clubs with no door policy or poncy dress codes, where anyone can get up to the DJ booth and spin a few tunes from their iPod. Tune!

HEY MR DJ

A new craze is sweeping clubland - 'MP3Jing'. Leave all your pretensions at the door

When Apple launched the third generation of iPods, they asked techno DJ Richie Hawtin to play an iPod set at their New York store. It wasn't as seamless as usual as you can't change pitch control to slow down or speed up tracks so they flow into each other yet (get with it, Mr Jobs!). But it is possible to play back-to-back songs using a mixer and two iPods - if your friend has an iPod, you can even do it at home - and set up parties where the emphasis is more on atmosphere and hearing unusual tunes than the skill of the DJ. This is the idea behind NoWax (geddit?), a club night that started off in 'London's trendy Hoxton' in July 2003 and has now spread to Manchester, Liverpool and Cardiff. MP3Jing has even reached New York and LA.

At NoWax, anyone can DJ. You just bring along your iPod, keep an eye on the overhead projector to find out when it's your turn and then get up and play three tracks. You 'mix' into the final song from the MP3J before you, then take turns to spin with the MP3J on next. Like the rap battles in Eminem's film *8 Mile*, you can react to what the person before you has just played. But you don't even have to do that - with up to 10,000 songs at your fingertips, you can choose whatever you like. Suddenly you're a superstar DJ who doesn't have to carry around back-breaking boxes of vinyl records. In fact, if you add up all the songs on all the iPods at a NoWax event, you're talking about half a million tunes in the room! Eat your heart out, Pete Tong.

'It's about having fun,' says NoWax organizer Raj Panjwani, an iPod obsessive since buying a 5GB model the first day it came out. 'It's exciting to hear what people are going to play next. At the end of the first night someone put on Dolly Parton and Kenny Rogers' 'Islands In the Stream', and everyone went mad. You can get away with anything. It's complete democracy - we don't censor music. Last time one guy played a tune he'd written himself. We're showing that digital music is a good thing because it exposes people to new types of music. It's not just a few sad geeks downloading stuff in their bedrooms - it's a real event.'

DJ and fellow organizer Charlie Gower came up with the idea for NoWax with Raj after mixing tunes from his iPod into vinyl during his sets. They wanted to recreate a similar atmosphere to that all-back-to-my-place spirit when everyone piles round someone's house and takes turns to put a CD on the stereo.

'It's been called

karaoke for people who can't sing,' says Charlie. 'People who never normally get to play tunes in bars or clubs are getting a taste of the glory - and they love it. When you're DJing with records, you're searching for another record all the time. With the iPod you just turn the wheel.' Enquiries have come in from people wanting to host NoWax nights from as far afield as Denmark, Paris, Italy, Kentucky, Florida and Tokyo.

Neil Williams organizes NoWax nights in Manchester, and Baby Cream in Liverpool. 'It's a really good atmosphere - the DJ booth is surrounded by people wanting to play,' he says. 'Someone played the *Airwolf* theme tune at the last NoWax and the whole place was singing along. Rather than one guy up there being all "Look at me, I'm the best DJ in town", everyone can be the best DJ in town and change the course of the night.'

MP3Jing has been a hit in America too - in one Los Angeles bar, people can plug their iPod into the sound system, while in New York, two guys calling themselves Andrew Andrew dress up in white labcoats and thick black-framed glasses to run their iParties on Tuesday nights in APT. MP3Js take a ticket from a deli dispenser and play a seven-minute set from a pre-selected 3,000 songs - an idea partly inspired by seeing Beck's iPod playlist in *The New York Times*. You don't even need to know how to use an iPod as they'll give you a quick tutorial before you go on. 'A lot of people would love to get into DJing, but it's difficult,' says, er, Andrew. 'Turntables and needles are very expensive. You can do a "bring your own vinyl" night but people are going to scratch vinyl, break needles and destroy turntables. The iPods offer an alternative. And, stylistically, they're aeons beyond vinyl.' Their iParties are so cool that superstar actor Elijah Wood (Frodo in *The Lord Of The Rings*) is a regular.

Andrew Andrew have now become celebrity DJs in their own right, playing out at other club venues and trendy gigs. Sometimes they even use iTunes's search function to play whole sets based on a single word - when they supported Chicks On Speed, every track they played had the word 'speed' either in the song title, artist name or lyrics. Another time, they played an entire forty-five minutes of cover versions of 'These Boots Were Made For Walkin''. So will we soon be seeing superstar DJs like Pete Tong and Fatboy Slim down the job centre? Not yet. In fact, iPods are the new best friend of Air-Mile-collecting DJs. Not many hotel rooms have a pair of turntables, but now DJs can digitize their vinyl on an iPod and use it when they're on the road to work out setlists and memorize intros and outros of records they've brought with them.

All this might change if Apple introduces mixing software for the iPod so that you can pitch bend, match BPMs, scratch, and queue up properly. You can already crossfade in iTunes so surely it's only a matter of time before it's introduced on the iPod. 'When Apple called me about the new iPod, I was like, "That's cool,"' says Richie Hawtin. 'But pitch control is what I really want. I could hook two iPods up to a mixer.' The possibilities for a professional DJ are endless. Apart from having enough tunes to exhaust even the most hyperactive clubber (a four-week rave, anyone?), they could even download a song from the Internet mid-gig while one track's playing and queue it up next. No more long hours spent browsing vinyl sections of record shops. Even without mixing software, NoWax's Neil is already hoping to take MP3Jing to the home of clubbing, Ibiza, through his connection with Cream. Raj is all for it. 'Big clubbing is dead - people are trying to create the party that you'd like to have back at your house,' he says. 'The iPod could become the Technics of the eighties and nineties.'

No Wax at DreambagsJaguarshoes, London; BabyCream, Liverpool; Centro, Manchester and Clwb Ifor Bach, Cardiff (www.nowax.co.uk)

PLAY

How to MP3J at home

All you need is a friend with an iPod, two 3.5mm jack-to-stereo leads and a mixer - pick up a cheap Numark or Gemini one for around £50 from music stores or buy second-hand. Then just connect the mixer to your home stereo. It's possible to roughly simulate scratch-ing and queueing up on an iPod by 'scrubbing' with the fast forward and rewind buttons - hold them down and your track will jump five seconds either way - but you have to be pretty nimble-fingered. You can also create playlists by beats per minute (BPM) in iTunes and then transfer them to your iPod. But if you want to be really professional, play your iPods through your computer while running a music-mixing program like Finalscratch or DJ Studio (www.hitsquad.com). Finalscratch allows real DJing with MP3s as it comes with an actual 12-inch record that's printed with code rather than music. By moving it on your turntable, it sends a signal to your computer to move the MP3 backwards or forwards so that you can scratch properly. Now all you need is some lino.

iSay . . .

'*You don't sit around any more saying, "If you dig that tune, you'll dig this too," you pull out your iPod instead and say, "Hey, listen to this."* ' **Max Valiquette, Toronto, Canada**

Hello, I Love You, Won't You Tell Me Your Name

Ipod's secret Cupid function revealed! The lovePod is a matchmaker too

Back in 5BI (Before the Internet), people used to mix cassette tapes to give to their boyfriends and girlfriends. Like John Cusack in *High Fidelity*, they'd use tracks that said something about the relationship and songs they thought their partner might like, as well as some personal favourites. Like an early example of peer-to-peer sharing, it was an insight into someone else's musical tastes that never failed to tell you more about their character and personality. Often it went horribly wrong, and you dumped them on the spot when you realized what a clue-less no-hoper they were.

Back in the twenty-first century, there's nothing that will tell you more about your crush than borrowing their iPod for an afternoon. Because listening to music on a personal stereo is such a private experience, they'll have way different tracks on their iPod to those they play on the stereo when you're round their house. You might find out your boyfriend's a secret Amy Winehouse fan and has a Smooth, Smooth Jazz playlist or that your girlfriend owns the entire Van Halen back catalogue. And if you can also get on to their PC to check out iTunes, there'll be no stone left unturned. It'll tell you the last track they listened to, their favourite songs (the Most Played list) and that while they claim The Streets are the best thing since, well, the iPod, they only own 'Weak Become Heroes' and have just played it twice. You see, the iPod don't lie.

But, while listening to your boyfriend or girlfriend's iPod might actually put you off them, it can also bring you closer as you discover a shared love of obscure twelve inches and those early Jamelia tracks. Complete strangers have fallen head over heels for each other, for when you see someone else wearing those white headphones, it's only natural to want to go up and talk to them and share your iPod love. It's like you're both part of some exclusive club. If you get on, soon you'll be wanting to plug your earphones into their iPod to see if you really are made for each other. In New York, iPod users are even starting to use personal ads to meet like-minded souls. One girl writes that she 'enjoys all the usual New York activities - like eating brie with raspberry jam and playing with my iPod'. And a guy who said he'd buy someone an iPod if they pretended to be his girlfriend for the night in front of his parents got forty replies. But most of the ads are from people trying to track down strangers wearing white earbuds they saw on the way to college or in the queue for the bus. Tall Asian Girl With Glasses writes, 'Where are you, my iPod man? I asked you about your iPod with the blue cover, and you just went ranting on about how the iPod is the invention of the century. You did not notice I was looking into your hazel eyes!' People aren't just in love with their iPods any more. They're in love with other people with iPods.

iSay . . .

'Since I started wearing the white ear-phones, seven strangers have come up to me. One girl asked what GB I had. When I said twenty, she said, "Oh I've got forty," and walked off!' Andy Sinclair, Glasgow

'Rival players just don't have the looks and style. Once I see the white cords, I find myself willing to talk to people. It's strange.' Namir Yedid, Maryland, USA

The Professor

Here's the science bit . . .

Thought you just liked listening to music? Wrong. According to Dr Michael Bull, you're 'controlling your mood and equilibrium and the space you move through'. A media and culture lecturer at Sussex Uni, Dr Bull has been researching the 'mobile music revolution' since 1979 and has now included the iPod in his studies. He became interested in personal stereos on holiday in Greece in 1992.

'I was on the beach and saw someone wearing a Sony Walkman. It struck me as strange because the surroundings were so beautiful and quiet and I couldn't understand why anyone would want to listen to anything else. It got me thinking about why people feel the need to change the soundscape they are in.

'I realized it gives people totally private worlds. Music on their personal stereos is often different to what they listen to at home, and reminds them of something nice. It's very personal and they don't want others listening to it. It's also very cinematic and allows you to construct narratives about what's going on. A lot of people don't like to be alone with their thoughts and the best way to avoid that is to listen to music.

'You never have to tune in to your environment. People can get on a bus or go shopping without having to interact with anyone else. People also become so immersed in listening it can take them a while to reorganize themselves back into the real world. Many use it for commuting. If you don't like where you're going in the day and can delay thinking about it until the last minute - people don't take their earphones off until they're inside the door - it's a great way to control mood and equilibrium.

'They will often play the same half-dozen songs for three months, and each part of the journey has its own tune. It gives them control of the space they're moving through and their interaction . . . For example, music allows people to use their eyes when they're listening in public. I call it nonreciprocal looking. The earplugs tell people you're otherwise engaged. A lot of women I spoke to felt safer with their earphones in. They can be the aural equivalent of sunglasses.

'On the positive side it allows people to reclaim their time for themselves. It also fits in with general cultural trends - doing things when you want. With the iPod, you have your music when you want it. And they're having a good time. Listening to music you like is the most effective way to make yourself feel better.

'With vinyl records, the aesthetic was in the sleeve, the artwork and the liner notes. With digital, the aesthetic is in the artefact - the iPod, not the music. It's moved from the disc to what you play it on. Half the people I've talked to so far download music illegally. The investment they're making is going into the artefact, not the music.

'The iPod is the first cultural icon of the twenty-first century. There is nothing else like it in terms of the mix of style, functionality and consumer desire. Music is the most powerful medium for thought, mood and movement control. The iPod will change the way people experience music in urban space. It allows users to listen to whatever they want non-stop, providing a soundtrack to their world.'

Fill in Dr Bull's questionaire by emailing him at M.Bull@sussex.ac.uk

iSay . . .

'With earphones in, I see people and don't hear them, so I think they're much nicer than they probably are.'
Anon

'You've got your biker community, your hip-hop community and now you've got your iPod commu-nity. It's all about those wires.'
Peterpaul Scott, New York, USA

Don't You Know Who i Am?

Celebs wouldn't be seen dead without an iPod

When the King and Queen of England, David and Victoria Beckham, were photographed wearing white headphones - Goldenballs while out jog-ging and Posh in New York - it was clear that iPods had been installed as the rightful heir to the MP3-player throne. And any lingering doubts were laughed off when Apple began selling limited edition engraved iPods signed by the Queen Mum, Madonna, as well as loyal subjects Beck, Tony Hawk and No Doubt (they're not available any more, sadly - but keep an eye out for new devotees). The country's second couple, Chris Martin and Gwyneth Paltrow, lent their support too. With Gwynnie telling magazines that she loves her iPod because it helps get her in the right mood for filming emotional scenes (not that we thought she'd need much help) and hubby Chris a self-proclaimed Machead, surely it's not just coincidence that the couple named their first child Apple?

Yes, it seems the iPod has become the latest essential celebrity accessory. Personal bodyguard? Check. Designer shades? Check. iPod? Check. Right, where's the red carpet? England's reluctant crown prince Jude Law uses his to relax during filming and Puerto Rican princess J.Lo gave her iPod the lead role in her 'Jenny From the Block' video. Future king Daniel Radcliffe (aka Harry Potter) became inseparable from his iPod on the set of *Prisoner Of Azkaban*, people's champion James Nesbitt takes his travelling and revolutionary Johnny Knoxville turned up at the Beverly Hills premiere of *Jackass: The Movie* wearing his. Rumours that he was listening to the *Love, Actually* soundtrack are unconfirmed. According to the gossip mags, other fully paid-up members of the iPod Hall of Fame include Daniel Bedingfield, Fatboy Slim, Franz Ferdinand, Goldie, Jack Osbourne, Nicole Kidman, Ricky Gervais, Ryan Adams and Kylie. Presumably she can't get 'i' out of her head (sorry). And when Apple launched the iPod Advent campaign (twenty-eight days of continuous new tunes from the 40GB) at the Virgin Megastore in London's Oxford Street for Christmas 2003, Irish prime minister Ronan Keating volunteered to press play. 'My iPod has become my travelling companion,' he said. 'It goes with me absolutely everywhere.'

American visionary Moby even discussed the idea of an iPod with Apple in a meeting about an iTunes prototype. Now he's got his wish, he loads his iPod up with sequences, samples, loops and bits of melody written on his home computer and takes them on late-night walks to sort into finished tracks. But while making your own tunes is one thing, losing them is every iPodder's worst nightmare. Even if they're mega-rich celebs. Poor old Michelle Branch had her iPod stolen when burglars raided her home. And Icelandic Queen Bjork got into a right old state when she thought she'd left hers in a trendy New York bar. Owner John Libonati says, 'Her people rang us four times.' Without any music, it seemed that Bjork's 1995 hit 'It's Oh So Quiet' had come back to haunt her. Until she found her iPod in her car four days later and rang up the bar to apologize. We love a happy ending.

On Blink 182's iPod:

'Hey You' - *Pink Floyd* ('The Wall')

'Push' - *The Cure* ('The Head on the Door')

'Tone Poem' - *Fischerspooner* (#1)

'Tropical London' - *Rancid* ('Indestructible')

'The Future Freaks Me Out' - *Motion City Soundtrack* ('I am the Movie')

'Happy' - *Ned's Atomic Dustbin* ('God Fodder')

'Flip Flop Rock' - *OutKast feat. Jay-Z and Killer Mike* ('Speakerboxxx/The Love Below')

'Such Great Heights' - *The Postal Service* ('Give Up')

'12:51' - *The Strokes* ('Room on Fire')

'Lebanese Blonde' - *Thievery Corporation* ('The Mirror Conspiracy')

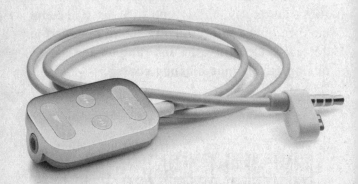

⏮ MENU ▶ ❚❚ ⏭

On Beyonce's iPod:

'A Song For You' - *Donny Hathaway* ('A Donny Hathaway Collection)

'Sun Will Shine Again' - *Michelle Williams* ('Heart to Yours')

'Crush' - *Solange* ('Solo Star')

'Train on a Track' - *Kelly Rowland* ('Simply Deep')

'Shackles (Praise You)' - *Mary Mary* ('Thankful')

'A Natural Woman' - *Aretha Franklin, Carole King, Celine Dion, Gloria Estefan, Mariah Carey, Shania Twain* ('VH1 Divas Live')

'Your Body is a Wonderland' - *John Mayer* ('Room for Squares')

'Stole' - *Kelly Rowland* ('Simply Deep')

'Kiss' - *Prince* ('The Hits/The B-sides')

'Rainy Day' - *Shuggie Otis* ('World Psychedelic Classics 2: California Soul – Inspiration Information')

myPod

Chapter 7 >

More Than That

Other stuff you can do with your iPod besides play music

While the iPod's extremely beautiful and you could mount it on your wall and stare at it for days, it's not just a pretty face. By now you should at least have realized that you can play music on your iPod (duh!). And you've probably already worked out that you can use it to tell the time, wake you up (although you'd have to be a pretty light sleeper as the alarm's dead quiet unless you put it through some speakers) and even send you off to the land of nod by setting the Sleep Timer. So here we'll concentrate on some of the cooler things you can do, like listening to audio books and stand-up comedy, playing games and storing phone numbers, email addresses and digital photos.

AUDIO BOOKS

You mean we don't actually have to read any more?

Audible is the Shakespeare play to everyone else's 'What I Did On My Summer Holidays' essay: way ahead of the competition when it comes to downloadable audio. The digital Bard (www.audible.com) has over 18,000 items of spoken word, including stand-up comedy from Robin Williams and Adam Sandler, authors reading their own short stories, newspapers like *The New York Times*, magazine articles, exclusive interviews, drama, poetry, radio shows and even relationship advice. But let's not forget what it's really about - audio books, all 6,000 of them. From modern-day novels like The Da Vinci Code to literary classics like Tolstoy's Anna Karenina, anti-corporate best-sellers like Fast Food Nation, through to science, history and economics textbooks and audio books for learning languages like Spanish and French, which beat traditional written textbooks hands down.

You get a ninety-second free sample, books start at about £5 and there are no stuffy librarians telling you to shhhhssssh. All Audible titles come with automatic bookmarking, which means that when you do eventually have to turn off your iPod, like to go to sleep for a few hours (shame on you), it picks up at exactly the same position when you come back, even if it's a couple of weeks later. You can even keep bookmarks in several titles at once, and the settings aren't affected whether you listen to music in between or update your iPod from iTunes. As books are split up into segments, either by chapters or time, it's also possible to scroll from one section to the next. And as spoken word takes up nowhere near as much memory as music, entire tomes can be stored as a single file (although the famously long *War and Peace* - sixty-two hours - stretches to three!).

When you buy a book, it's kept in your Audible library forever, so if you lose it in a hard-disk pile-up, just nip back and 'borrow' it again. No fines for overdue books here. Download by first selecting a format and quality of file, rated from one to four (telephone to AM radio to FM radio to MP3). The higher the number, the better the quality but the longer it takes to download and the more space it uses up. It's just one of the rules of life. If you haven't got broadband, try format 2 or 3 (if there's any music in the audio, you'll need higher quality), although telephone quality is surprisingly good - test it on the site.

Thirty minutes of MP3-standard sound takes twenty-two minutes to download with a 56K modem or two and a half minutes with broadband. The file appears in an Audible folder on your hard disk - add it to iTunes by dragging and dropping or any other of the usual methods. Just like music, audio books are copy-protected, and some you can't copy to CD. Though why you'd want to when you can listen to them directly on your iPod is beyond us. You can also buy Audible books directly from the iTunes Music Store - although there's a choice of *only* 5,000 - current faves are Madonna reading her book, *The English Roses,* and J.R.R.

Tolkien's *The Hobbit*. They come in the AAC format but work in exactly the same way and download straight to the iTunes library.

Most of the alternatives to Audible aren't worth writing a book about. However, getting stuff for free is never, *ever* to be sniffed at, and a different matter entirely. At the UK's very own www.audiobooksforfree.com you can find MP3s of out-of-copyright classics by Joseph Conrad and Conan Doyle, Bram Stoker's *Dracula*, Robert Louis Stevenson's *Treasure Island* as well as children's books like *Alice in Wonderland*. The sound isn't great, but hey, there's the rub. There are also free audiobooks at the Project Gutenberg website (www.gutenberg.net). And worth a browse if you've got some coins in your pocket are PayPerListen (www.payperlisten.com), a similar, but smaller, site to Audible and Time Warner (www.mytimewarneraudio.com), which boasts the Dalai Lama's autobiography and a few other bestsellers in WMA. They don't come with bookmarks, but Mac users can save them as AAC and then run the iTunes Applescript (in the Scripts Menu) called Make Bookmarkable that . . . yup, you guessed it. Now, where were we?

RADIO SHOWS

Audioblogging could be the saviour of radio

With the advent of digital radio, times are a-changing for one of the oldest forms of media.

Even the lumbering BBC dinosaur has got in on the act by releasing some of its radio shows as MP3s. Unfortunately, the first ones were a load of boring lectures. What's far more exciting, though, is that the BBC has huge warehouses of music recorded over the thousands of years of its existence, including live sessions by everyone from The Beatles to Maroon 5. There's talk of allowing people to download programmes free for seven days, after which you can buy them permanently. Various other sites offer free MP3 downloads; you can listen to the archives of cool student station IC Radio (http://icradio.com/relive), for instance.

But what's way more ear-tingling is that you can now buy music directly off the radio the moment you hear it. Radio station Classic FM (don't turn the dial just yet!) was first with its revolutionary 'hear it, buy it, burn it' service, where online listeners to any of its 34 local stations can just click on the Buy button to legally download a CD-quality file of the song that's playing. It makes sense - radio is the way most of us hear new music - but now you don't even have to make the trip to the record store. Heart FM is already selling downloadable ringtones for mobile phones and plans to move on to singles next, while cooler, younger stations such as Emap, Capital and Chrysalis are in the mix too. And as record companies are now releasing songs to download as soon as they're played on the radio, there'll be no more yawnsome four-week waits until tracks are in the shops - by which time we're already bored of them anyway.

Back at Audible, downloadable radio programmes, such as recordings of American talk shows, comedy and exclusive broadcasts are the fastest growing part of its library. Next, Audible is going to experiment with selling DIY radio shows. Anyone can make them - all you need is some recording software and a cheap microphone and suddenly you're the new Chris Moyles. 'Audioblogging' or 'pocasting' is just the natural next step on from weblogging - some bloggers already have downloadable MP3 audio on their sites (www.audblog.com has the tech). So forget pirate radio - now everyone and anyone can (legally) have their own voice. Plus you can tell pretty quickly if you're on the same, ahem, wavelength as your listeners by checking to see how many people have clicked on your audioblog. If your show's really popular, you might actually be able to make a living out of it. You could even record it on a laptop on a Caribbean beach, upload it to the Internet and then your listeners back in England could download it to their iPods to play on the No. 73 bus. Video killed the radio star? Not any more.

GAMES

Apple makes work for idle thumbs

Early iPods came with just one game, Brick (the old knock-down-a-wall-with-a-bouncing-ball chestnut), but it was actually hidden and trying to find it was almost as much fun as actually playing. These days we've got four - there's the shoot-'em-down arcade game Parachute and the Never Mind the Buzzcocks-style Music Quiz, which gives you five seconds to guess a random snippet of one of the thousands of songs on your iPod from five possible answers. Points are awarded for how quickly you can spot the tune. Then there's the classic Solitaire, which is kinda fiddly and you might have to use the backlight to see the cards (especially on the mini). However, it should come in handy now that you've ditched all your friends in favour of your new toy.

Now software companies have even started to create extra iPod games so you need never interact with the outside world again. XO Play has a selection based on the Terry Prachett-style choose-your-own-adventure books, which you play through the notes function (£8 each, www.xoplay.com). In The Rise Of The Lost, you become Sir Jacob Zaviour, on a *Lord Of The Rings*-scale mission to seek out and fight Wizard Sazque, a real nasty piece of work. You quest is won or lost depending on the choices you make at the bottom of the page. And in Bum Rags To Riches, you're a tramp called Rufus, searching through dustbins and trying to scrape together enough coppers to escape the down-and-out life. As Del-Boy said in *Only Fools And Horses*: 'This time next year, Rodney . . . we're gonna be millyonaires.'

'I bought my iPod so I could listen to music while I'm skateboarding. But then I realized it's actually dead cool for carrying homework around and great for playing Solitaire on the toilet!' Tom Addick, Portsmouth

CONTACTS AND CALENDAR

'It looks like I've got a window next Tuesday'

Forgotten when that important work project or geography homework is due in? Just check your iPod. Oops, missed the deadline again! You can use your iPod like a mobile organizer or PDA by storing diary info and reminder alarms, email addresses, websites and phone numbers - even song lyrics and to-do lists (which you can then happily ignore). And while you're busy seeing if you can 'do lunch' next week, you can continue listening to your music.

When your iPod's connected to your computer, click on the Options button in the bottom left of the iTunes window and go to Enable Disk Use. You've just entered a whole new world. Open up the iPod folder on your desktop and you'll see the Calendar, Contacts and Notes folders (don't rename them or your iPod will get a severe headache). Drag and drop files into these folders from most email and address book applications - the iPod is compatible with Microsoft Outlook and

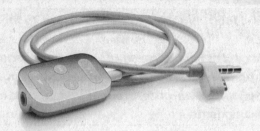

Entourage, Palm Desktop, Eudora and Address Book and recognizes vCalendar, iCalendar and vCard files. We don't want you to miss that important meeting with the new episode of *The O.C.*, so remember to always activate imported alarms on the iPod.

To make your life even more of a breeze, there are programs that do all the legwork for you. The Holy Grail is Apple's iSync, free from www.apple.com/isync, which automatically updates your calendar, contacts and to-do lists when you connect your iPod and also links up with Palm-style organizers and Bluetooth phones. Just go to Add Device and click on the iPod icon the first time you install iSync and you're off and away. If you're a Windows user, download software such as the free iAppoint (www.xs4all.nl/~hagemans) or iPodSync (£7, www.ipodlounge.com). EphPod and OutPod also work with Microsoft Outlook while Palm2iPod does the business with Palm Desktop (all free). When you've got your life in order, remember that as you're using the iPod as a hard disk, you need to eject it manually. Like you're a nightclub bouncer.

NOTES

Say goodbye to scribbles on scraps of paper and backs of bus tickets

In a digital world where the only thing a pen is useful for is rebooting your PMU, the Notes function allows you to view your brainwaves and things-to-do lists on the hoof. Because of the iPod's relatively small screen, you can't view much text (six lines at a time on the mini) so Notes are more suited to small files like extra album info, song lyrics, that day's horoscope or even your maths homework. You can even read them in the dark with the backlight (press and hold the Menu button). Save small word files as ordinary text (extension .txt) or use TextEdit on the Mac or Notepad in Windows. As ever, there are various software and Applescripts that allow you to do fancy things, like iLyric for the Mac (www.ipod-lounge.com), which searches the Internet for those heartfelt words of wisdom from your fave artists and copies them to the iPod. Various Applescripts such as Clipboard To Notes, Clear All Notes, List Notes and Printer Friendly (for grabbing text from web pages) can be found free at www.apple.com/apple-script/ipod. Each Note file is only 4KB, but you can link them together so you can read longer documents if you've got the scrolling skills of a concert pianist and the patience of a particularly chilled Trappist monk. Book2Pod for Macs splits up text into the right size (free, www.ipodlounge.com). Or, if you want to catch up with the outside world and find out when Brad Pitt's next in town, Windows program GoogleGet downloads news straight to your iPod (free, www.ipodlounge.com).

iSay . . .

'*I've encoded and saved all my website passwords on my iPod because I can never remember them all.*' Raj Panjwani, London

'*The iPod will change your life. You can back up school projects, have extra copies of your papers on there and still have plenty of room for music. I don't even think I have ten thousand songs I like!*' Shawn Beatty, Ohio, USA

HARD DISK STORAGE

Why the iPod should have won an Oscar

Next time anyone starts dissing your iPod as being an expensive fashion statement that plays a few tunes (what's wrong with that, anyway?), this should shut them right up. The iPod is essentially a hard drive. Which means that you can use it in exactly the same way as your computer - except it's way more portable so you can transfer data until the cows come home. And even after they go back out again. You can store word documents such as presentations, speeches and English essays, printer drivers, fonts and whole applications such as Photoshop and email programs to take between home and work or college to make life easier when you're using a different computer. Not only that, but on bigger iPods you can store hundreds of digital photos (see the Belkin Media Reader in chapter eight), and even store the Mac's operating system so you can reboot from your iPod should your computer have a funny turn.

Still not convinced? True story time. During the making of *The Lord of the Rings: The Two Towers* and *The Return of the King*, the production team used a 30GB iPod to transfer data from the film studio in New Zealand to director Peter Jackson's London home. Visual effects, sequences, miniatures and raw footage were stored as 1K-resolution QuickTime files, beamed over the Internet from Wellington to Pinewood Studios in London, transferred to Sir's iPod and delivered to his door. The director would then connect the iPod to his laptop to view the files and give the thumbs up or down through a video-conferencing line to New Zealand. Much of the Pelanor battle sequence was finalized in this way, and seeing as *The Return of the King* won eleven Oscars, we reckon the iPod deserves at least one for its trouble.

So what do you have to do to access this whole new hidden kingdom? Just go to Enable Disk Use by clicking on the Options button at the bottom right corner of iTunes and you're good to go. Open up the iPod folder on your desktop and drag and drop files, folders and applications into the window. Remember, though, you can't read word documents, view digital photos or watch movie clips directly on your iPod - this is all about transferring files from one computer to another by sneaker net (that's you on foot, fool). And in that respect, your iPod is the lightest, most stylish briefcase in the world. Maybe that's why *Newsday* in New York called the iPod 'the Louis Vuitton of portable audio'.

i'M a celebrity: Film director Anthony Minghella (*The Talented Mr Ripley, Cold Mountain*):

'I can't live without my iPod. It's filled with Bach and about three hundred tracks of American Civil War-era music, which I listened to during twelve months in Romania filming Cold Mountain. When I really want to tune everything out, I listen on my Bose noise-cancelling headphones.'

i'M a celebrity: Sci-fi author Iain Banks

'My latest toy is the 20GB iPod. I wonder when I'm ever going to find time to listen to all the weird stuff I've been filling it up with.

iSay . . .

'I've got about a hundred and fifty digital photos and a bootable version of Mac OS X on my 20GB iPod - my laptop is only 20GB! And I got some software from iPodlounge to put Outlook on it so I can read my emails whenever I want. It's like a PDA.'

Neil Williams, Manchester

DID YOU KNOW?
The world's weirdest iPod uses

Flying high

Business-types can listen to a 40GB iPod as they wait for their flight in Virgin Atlantic's Upper Class lounges at Heathrow airport in London and JFK, New York. The suits' top choices are Red Hot Chili Peppers, R.E.M. and, er, The Darkness. Lock to rock!

Free car with your iPod, sir?

Parents thinking about replacing the family motor? Three car companies have all come up with limited-edition iPod-friendly models. In the US, there's the Volkswagen Beetle that comes with special wiring and a cradle, plus the 'iPod ready' Alpine in which you can use the car stereo (or its wireless remote) to scroll through playlists and charge your iPod while it's safely tucked up in bed in the glove compartment. But the gold star goes to the UK's Smart fortwo i-move that actually comes with a free 20GB iPod, mounted on its own docking station. Yours for just £12,500. That's only two and a half pence a tune!

A work of art

The Japanese have always been one technological step ahead. Last February visitors to Toyko's Mori Art Museum were lent 20GB iPods to listen to an audio guide of a contemporary exhibition. Whatever next? Oh, hang on . . .

Praise the Lord!

Most of us are guilty of some kind of iPod worship, but what about actually worshipping *with* your iPod? At one church in Alpharetta, USA, hymns and church music are actually loaded on to an iPod and played before and after the service. Hallelujah!

HEY, MAMA

How to persuade your parents to get you an iPod

It's good for your back

Tell them you can use the iPod to take your homework to and from school, not to mention store audio economics, history, science and language textbooks from Audible to save you having to lug around a schoolbag laden down with heavy books and files

You've seen the light

They don't take you to church any more (NB, this is a guilt-trip that might backfire) and you want to catch up on your religious education with BiblePod (free, www.ipod-lounge.com), which transfers chapters from the Great Book on to your machine

To Pod or not to Pod, that is the question

You can get some software at www.ipodhacks.com that will deliver a Shakespeare sonnet to your iPod each day. Which will naturally propel you to the top of the class in English Lit

Practice makes perfect

You're in the school choir or orchestra and want to use the iPod to listen to the piece you're performing to help learn your part

It'll teach you long-term financial management

If they set up a direct debit to put, let's say . . . £10 into your iTunes Music Store Allowance Account each month, it'll force you to learn how to manage your cash and spread out your downloading purchases. Which will of course be invaluable when you go to university and have to live off student loans.

However, If none of this works, you might have to resort to the old 'But, *Muuuuuuum*, everyone else has got one' line . . .

myPod

Chapter 8   >

She's in Fashion

Accessorise, accessorise

The iPod has given birth to over 300 add-ons and fashion accessories with major companies such as Griffin, Belkin, Monster Cable and Digital Lifestyle Outfitters employing thousands of people between them. One company even makes a case for another firm's speakers so now there are accessories for accessories. It seems that once people fall in love with their iPod they like to treat it, like buying dog collars and fancy kennels for the family pet. And why not? Your iPod accompanies you everywhere so naturally you'll want to take good care of it and find add-ons that allow you to plug it in wherever you are. And while the iPod's design is super-stylish in itself, as more and more iPods appear on the streets, people want to make theirs stand out from the crowd. So here's a list of our favourites. And also some that are just downright weird. (Note that while you may find some accessories cheaper on US websites, you'll have to pay for shipping and wait longer for them to arrive.)

HEADPHONES
(mini, original)

Yes, your iPod comes with a lovely white pair of earbuds that provide a great sound. But that doesn't mean you can't get some cool new ones. There is an endless choice and we'd need another book to mention them all. Apple's online store has In-Ear Headphones for different sized lugholes (although these have been criticized for their bass response) but any pair will fit the iPod so long as they have a 3.5mm jack. And if your parents kick up a stink and ask why you need another pair, tell them that kids have been mugged for wearing white ones. That should get them down the shop pretty sharpish.

BARGAIN: Sennheiser MX 500
These tiny metallic-blue in-ear headphones have great sound and wind back into the case when you're not using them so you don't get all tangled up (£20, www.everythingipod.co.uk). The black and silver MX 400s are slightly lower in quality but even cheaper (£15, www.sennheiser.co.uk)

IN YOUR DREAMS: ER-6 Isolator Headphones
Noise-cancelling in-ear headphones so good they're almost dangerous - you won't be able to hear anything going on around you (£85, www.etymotic.com).

Smartwrap Headphone Cord Manager
Say goodbye to headphones tangles - just

wrap any extra wiring around this cool double-notched plastic contraption. It comes in eight colours so you can accessorize with your mini or outfit (£4, ww.ipodx.co.uk/products/sumajin_smartwrap.shtml).

Headphone splitter
Share your music with your best mate using a Y cable. One end connects to your headphone socket while the other divides in two so that you can both plug in your earbuds. Just make sure it's a good quality splitter, otherwise one of you will get much better sound and there'll be tears before bedtime. Try the Bellein Headphone splitter (£10, http://store.apple.com)

PORTABLE SPEAKERS

(original, mini)
Because sometimes you just want to share your music with the world. If you've already got a pair of speakers that you use for your Walkman, they'll fit your iPod. If you're buying new ones, decide what you're going to use them for. Get travel-sized ones to take away or good power output and a booming bass to throw an iParty.

BARGAIN: Sony SRS-T55 Personal Travel Speakers
Brilliant flip-out speaker set that fits in your hand with a great combo of sound and portability. Gets its (surprisingly fruity) juice from four AA batteries (£35, www.amazon.co.uk).

MID-RANGE: Creative TravelSound

Cool-looking silver and black travel speakers with a really clean sound, headphone jack, wide stereo effects and volume control. Runs off a power adaptor or for thirty-five hours from four AAA batteries (£49, http://store.apple.com).

IN YOUR DREAMS: Altec Lansing inMotion Portable Audio System

Designed specifically for the iPod, the white inMotion speakers are super-stylish. Your iPod slots into a standard dock (that allows you to do all the normal functions) between the speakers and is powered by an AC adaptor or four AA batteries that will last for twenty-four hours. It weighs just 15oz and folds up to the size of a hardcover book and you can now get a free adaptor for the mini. The sound isn't the best ever, but, hey, it's got an alarm clock and looks very cool (£99, http://store.apple.com).

WEIRD: JBL Creature II

They're not portable but are so unusual that we thought we'd include them anyway. In iPod white, there are three speakers - a subwoofer and two desktop speakers that look like a family of aliens. Especially when they're lit up with the green LEDs (£70, www.every thingipod.co.uk).

DON'T TRY THIS AT HOME: FM RADIO TRANSMITTER

(original, mini)

Weird one, this. FM transmitters plug into your iPod and beam tunes to the nearest radio receiver. So you can play the iPod wirelessly through your home hi-fi, car stereo, a portable radio down the park or on the beach or clock radio in a hotel room. Just tune the radio in to the right frequency. Absolute genius. But the use of FM transmitters, like top-selling iPod accessory the Griffin iTrip and the Belkin TuneCast II, is banned in the UK for the out-of-touch reason that they could interfere with official broadcasts and be used for pirate radio stations - even though they only work over a few metres. It's time for the law to catch up with technology. Get with it, m'lud!

FM RADIO RECEIVER

(original, mini)

Got thousands of tunes but still want to hear more? Listen to the radio directly on your iPod with the FM-Xtra 5430 - a stereo auto-scan FM radio in a pair of headphones (£18, www.iskins.co.uk)

REMOTE CONTROLS

You don't want to have your iPod by your side all the time - people might start to talk. So shut them up while you relax in the comfort of your armchair with a wireless remote.

SAME ROOM: naviPod
(original)
One beautiful piece of kit. The white receiver plugs into the top of your iPod and is attached to a chrome stand which props your machine up. Plug your stereo or portable speakers into the back and control the iPod with the disc-like infrared remote (£35, http://store.apple.com).

ROUND CORNERS: RemoteRemote 2
(original, mini)
The cylinder-like white RemoteRemote 2 sits on top of your iPod and not only provides wireless control around corners but through walls too. Change volume and navigate from the keyfob, which comes in either black or white. Should be available in the UK soon. (£25, www.engineeredaudio.com)

OUT OF THIS WORLD: naviPlay
(original)
Now the future really is upon us. One of the very first Bluetooth-enabled accessories, the naviPlay allows you to get rid of your earphone cords once and for all. The transmitter plugs into the iPod and the adaptor connects with most types of headphones and speakers. It has an LCD display and buttons for remote control as well as scrolling through menus and

playlists. If you already have a Bluetooth headset for your mobile (very flash), you can now answer calls and listen to your music through the same piece of kit. Although not at the same time. That would be silly (coming soon, deets at www.tentechnology.com).

VOICE RECORDER
(original)

Microphones for recording voice memos, live gigs, band practices, sound effects, interviews and lectures (so you can fall asleep at the back) were some of the most eagerly awaited add-ons. Recordings are saved in Extras>Voice Memos as WAV files and named by the date and time created. Store thousands of hours on the iPod or transfer to your computer for editing or emailing to friends. You can even use recordings as an alarm - wake yourself up with your own voice shouting, 'Get out of bed, lazy!' or the soothing tones of your mum telling you she's made you a cuppa.

The Griffin iTalk plugs into the top of your iPod and claims to be able to record up to thirty metres away. It has a built-in microphone but you can also attach an external mic for higher quality. Alternatively, attach your earbuds to listen as you record to make sure it's not dis-torted or listen to music with the iTalk still attached. The built-in speaker can even play your tunes (£29, http://store.apple.com).

*'I've got outtakes and off-mike comments
from my recording sessions with P Diddy.
Those, plus my entire studio sessions, take
up most of my iPod space.'*

CASES

There are more cases than all the other accessories put together. Not surprising, really,
because everyone wants to protect the one they
love. And as iPods are so small, it's very easy for
them to get dirty and scratched in pockets and
handbags, while fingerprint marks are the bane of
any careful owner's life. There are invisible
sleeves, super-light coloured skins, wipeout-
resistant bricks for skateboarders, waterproof
ones, furry ones, crocheted ones, businessy
Filofax-style leather holders, those that hang
round your neck or over your shoulder,
cases that double as stands and even holsters
from top designers like Prada and
Emilio Pucci. Try www.everythingipod.co.uk,
www.ipodlounge.com, www.amazon.co.uk,
www.drbott.com, www.xtrememac.com and
www.marware.com for starters. And if you find
your dream case on a US site that doesn't ship to
the UK, try your luck on ebay. The choice, as they
say, is yours.

**INVISIBLE: Pod Shield
(original)**
Transparent film that clings to your iPod by

static - no glue or residue marks here. So when they need replacing, just peel off. Great if you want to continue to show off the beautiful design of the iPod while keeping it pristine and free from ugly scratches (£8 for three, www.ipodx.co.uk).

SWITCH COLOUR: iSkin (original, mini)

Ultralight moisture-proof protective covering that comes in forty different colours - so you can change the colour of your mini if you couldn't get the one you wanted in the first place. Some iSkins even glow in the dark. The back has pores to dissipate heat, there are goosebumps for grip and openings for all sockets (£23 or £22 for the mini, www.iskins.co.uk). Still not satisfied? Spice up white iPods even more with iShades - transparent panels for the screen in shades like Emerald, Rose and Indigo Light (£2.50, www.iskins.co.uk).

CAMOUFLAGE: PodSkinz iPod Faceplate Covers (original)

Pack of three unusual designs like Pop Art, Camouflage and Skulls that stick on to the front and protect at the same time. Plus they're easy to remove so you can swap whenever you like (£22 plus shipping, www.every-thingipod.com).

PRINTS: SportSuit Safari (mini)

Furry animal-print cases in designs like Zebra and Giraffe. Come with a black strap for the shoulder or wrist. Miaow! (£11 plus shipping, www.marware.com).

CUTE: Chuckles Central iPod Cozies (original, mini)
Get a handmade crocheted bunny or pooch case for your kid sister. Aw. (£10 plus shipping, www.chucklescentral.com).

BEACH: Zipod (original, mini)
Take your iPod on hols without worrying about getting sand or seawater in it by zipping it in a transparent, waterproof case. Pass the suncream. (£7 plus shipping, www.thinkdifferentstore.com).

WAR ZONE: iPod Armour (original, mini)
If you're a skateboarder or a snowboarder, or just incredibly accident-prone, the Armour covers your machine completely in a wipe-out-proof white aluminium case (you can still access the ports) while wrapping it up in a soft foam cocoon to absorb shocks. Ah. (£34.99, www.everythingipod.co.uk).

TOUR OF DUTY: Xtremity iPod Accessory System (original)
Nearly as strong as the Armour but much cheaper. Some devotees also like the fact that it connects to belt clips and mounts (which it comes with) through two grooves down the back so that it lies perfectly flat

when loose. Plus the removable front panel flips up. Which is kinda cool (£17 plus shipping, www.xtrememac.com).

STYLISH: DLO Podsling Leather iPod Carryall Case (original)
Leave the belt clips to builders and IT geeks - the only way to carry your iPod this season is with a red or black hand-stitched Italian leather Podsling, dahling. It straps over your shoulder so the iPod sits on your waist in a pouch with pockets for cards and earbuds (£22 plus shipping, www.everythingipod.com).

IN YOUR DREAMS: Dior Homme iPod Case and Gucci iPod case (original)
Even designers like Emilio Pucci, Prada, Dior and Gucci got in on the act. The Dior Homme printed leather cover comes with a belt loop or leather shoulder strap in black, pale pink and khaki. And the really quite stylish beige/ebony Gucci holster with dark leather trim has the signature logo and a green-and-red striped strap. But it's wasted on fashionistas - they might be able to work a room but when it comes to technology, they couldn't work the timer on a video (www.dior.com or www.gucci.com).

ARMBANDS AND WRISTBANDS
(original, mini)
These are for sporty types who like to take their iPod jogging or down the gym. Well, there's no point in letting that twenty-five-minute skip protection go to waste, is

there? The DLO Action Jacket comes in four different colours and attaches to your arm with Velcro (start working on those biceps!). Operate the buttons and touchwheel through the transparent screen (£24, www.everythingipod.co.uk). You can also wear your iPod like a giant watch. DLO also sells coloured elastic and Velcro wristbands that fit to the Action Jacket mini (£5 plus shipping, www.everythingipod.com). Or try Marware's SportSuit Runabout that has a shell to protect your mini from jarring. So when you fall down that pothole and break your ankle, your iPod will still be playing away obliviously (£22, www.amazon.co.uk).

CLEANERS
(original, mini)
There's really no need to splash the cash on a cleaning product for your iPod - just use a glasses or camera-lens cloth. But if you thought you'd save some money by not buying a case and now you've got a diagonal scar right across the back or black smudges all over the front, bet you're feeling a bit silly. Still, you could always try one of these products.
*The iCleaner Pro Scratch Remover (£15, www.amazon.co.uk) takes care of white iPods' plastic
*Klear Screen wipes (£9.50 for pack of twelve, www.amazon.co.uk) polish up your display.

DOCK
(original, mini)
The 20GB and the mini don't come with

a dock but don't start getting jealous of your big brutha. Docks are more of a luxury than anything, especially if you've got a mini because it charges directly from your computer. You can use the dock to connect to your stereo, but then you can do the same thing with a cheap cable. So use your money to buy some tunes instead.

STORING DIGITAL PHOTOS
(original)

People used to carry passport photos of loved ones in their wallets (your parents have probably still got one of you as a baby. Ew) and now you can do it on your iPod. The hard disk can store hundreds of photos - of your holiday or that party last week - so you can take them walkies to plug in and show your friends wherever you like. Or use your iPod to free up the memory on your digital camera. Transfer photos over FireWire from a media card with the Belkin Media Reader (£90, www.every-thingipod.co.uk) or via a USB link direct to your camera with the Belkin Digital Camera Link (£80, www.amazon.co.uk). Then, when you get home, connect your iPod to your computer to retrieve the images. Da na!

BACK-UP BATTERY PACK
(original)

If you're thinking about running away and leaving modern civilization behind, you're naturally going to want to take your iPod with you to while away the hours on that desert island. Enter the Belkin Back-up Battery Pack, which powers your iPod using four standard AA batteries (better make sure you take a big old supply) that give you fifteen to twenty extra hours of playing time. It's also very handy if you're into prog rock, allowing you to listen to at least three tracks. The Pack attaches limpet-like on to the back of the iPod with suction cups, and LED indicators let you know when to replace the batteries. Now you can really mean it when you say, 'I'm going out. I may be some time . . .' (£44, www.everythingipod.co.uk)

IN-CAR ACCESSORIES
(original, mini)

The easiest (and clearest) way to play your iPod through a car stereo is with an FM transmitter. But they're, like, illegal, so here's how you can do it without getting your shoulder felt by PC Plod. Thank your lucky stars if your motor has a socket for connecting iPods directly - you're obviously one of the chosen ones. Otherwise, use a standard cassette adaptor from any electrical store to play through the tape deck. A wire pokes out and connects to your iPod. Clean the player regularly with a special tape otherwise the sound will get muffled. You can also charge your iPod (or mobile or laptop) through the cigarette lighter. Again a standard adaptor from an electrical shop will be cheaper and just as efficient as any, but if you want to keep that white theme going, all the iPod accessory companies make them. Now all you need is a car.

i'M a celebrity: Robbie Williams

> '*I've got three and a half thousand songs on this little white box that I put in my car and play - it's amazing.*'

ER, CLOTHING -
(original, mini)

Yes, the iPod has even infiltrated the world of fashion. You'll have heard of that famous *Lord of the Rings* T-shirt, you know, the one with Gollum hugging an iPod saying, 'My precious'? Get it, and others, at www.tshirts.com/stores/?id=16320352 in various styles and colours (£12, plus shipping). Or there's the iPod Culture tee that has an iPod print on the front and the cheeky 'What's in your pocket?' on the back (£15, www.everythingipod.co.uk).

Burton makes a range of snowboard gear so you can listen to Air as you grab some. Jackets have a special iPod pocket and a built-in control pad on the sleeve so you can change playlists without fumbling around with zips and pockets - even while wearing mittens! And the Burton Amp Pack is the world's first backpack with an iPod control system. Not that there was much competition. Tuck your baby into the secure storage pocket, and control it through a flexible pad on the shoulder strap, which also has an earbud port. Crank it up for the slopes, then turn it down to chat to your boarding buddies on the lift. You might not be able to afford a ski pass after buying one, though (www.burton.com).

From here on in things start to get distinctly weird. Savile Row-type Pal Zileri has designed a suit jacket with an anti-sag pocket sewn into the lining for white iPods and white silk loops up the inside of the lapel for wires. It's only £799. And don't even get us started on Felicidade's catchily named Groove Bag Triplet Speaker Purse. Someone's actually spent hundreds of hours designing and producing this white PVC iPod handbag with a cut-out handle. The iPod slips into a central outward-facing pocket between a pair of built-in speakers. Not content with that, Felicidade has come up with an alternative version, the Groove Purse Tote, which looks like more of a shopper and has leather handles for what they call the 'about town' look. Er, whatever. (£103, www.amazon.co.uk)

DIYPOD

Want to really stand out from the crowd? Customize your iPod

For that truly personal touch, ColorWare will handpaint your iPod in 24 colours (£27 plus shipping) and even match accessories like earbuds for a little extra (www.color-warepc.com). Or you could cover your iPod with cool stickers from places like Paperchase, Woollies or off the Internet. At www.ipodmods.com you can change the colour of the white iPod's display to blue, white, green or orange (£50 plus shipping). But for the true individual, get it engraved.

When you buy an iPod from Apple online, you can etch its name (you have named it, right?) or any message into the silver case for free. Only problem is, Apple have been known to reject engravings like '10,000 Stolen Tunes Inside'. The solution? Just take it down to your local jeweller and get them to do it for you. Check out the Virtual Engraving facility at www.ipodlaughs.com for inspiration with classics like: 'Devil has my soul. I have iPod. I did well' and 'If found, please return to . . . who am I kidding?'

THE IPODLOUNGE

It might be a website, but it's still an essential accessory for any discerning iPod owner

Set up by Los Angeleno Dennis Lloyd two and a half years ago after losing his job as a web designer, the mixture of news, humour, reviews, accessories, tips and tricks, software and freeware downloads soon meant he didn't have to go back to the nine-to-five. With 4 million visitors a month and counting and 12,000 people registered in the discussion forum, he's pretty much got his hands full with iPods. Much like yourself. 'We've created a global online community,' he says. 'People love their iPods and want to share their experience with other users.' In one of the funniest parts of the site, the iPods

Around The World photo gallery, owners have uploaded 2,500 holiday snaps of iPods relaxing in over sixty countries from the UK to China, and the pyramids to jungle expeditions in Peru, like the kidnapped gnome in *Amélie*. There are photos of iPods 275 metres below the earth's surface, on top of mountains and sunbathing on beaches in Greece and Florida. There are even pictures of Darth Vader and a dog on a motorbike wearing one, plus a rather convincing Stonehenge constructed out of iPods. 'I'm surprised it's been so successful,' says Dennis. 'But I had a feeling the iPod would take the world by storm.'

BATTERIES NOT INCLUDED

Five things that should have come with your iPod

- **Medical kit.**
  So you can surgically insert those earbuds
- **A warning.**
  Like they have on ciggie packets: 'The iPod Can Seriously Damage Your Social Life'
- **Plasters.**
  To cover up the blisters on your scrolling hand
- **Do Not Disturb sign.**
  Attached halfway down your earbud cords so that no one bothers you when you're listenin'
- **Er . . . another iPod?**
  Well, there's no harm in asking

iSay . . .

'I took my iPod on holiday and played it through some mini speakers I picked up at the airport. I put it on shuffle and didn't hear the same song twice.' Andy Greenhouse, London

'When I get home at night the first thing I do is plug my iPod in to make sure I have battery power for the next day. It's almost like your iPod becomes an extension of you. I suppose I'm a bit of a fanatic.' Aaron Ladage, Iowa, USA

myPod

Chapter 9 >

Trouble

How to solve common iPod problems

Wipe away those tears because things are never as bad as they seem. Don't consign your iPod to the graveyard in the sky just yet - most problems can be easily fixed. Firstly, for those of you who still haven't worked out how to stop sending TEXTS IN CAPITALS, here are a few basic facts and simple things to check.

1. If your iPod won't turn on, check the Hold switch. Or it might be because it's run out of juice - charge it up from the adaptor.

2. The iPod doesn't like very cold or hot environments - like the glove compartment of a car on a sunny day. Or it could literally be freezing and refuse to wake up. Wait until it's cooled down or heated up (holding it in your hand for a few minutes should work) and try again.

3. When you're connecting cables, the symbol should face upwards. Keep them protected with the plastic covers when not in use to prevent dust getting in there.

4. Your iPod can't charge from a computer that's asleep.

5. Some problems can be solved simply by turning your computer off and disconnecting the iPod for a couple of minutes before restarting.

6. Don't use a Disk Utility program on your iPod. Then you really will be in trouble.

7.Make sure you've got enough hard disk space for all your music. MP3 files take up roughly 4MB each.

8. Don't be alarmed if your iPod seems to have 0.3GB less hard disk space than it should. This is used up by the iPod's operating system.

9. Still having nightmares? Read on for more advanced trouble-shooting techniques that should ensure you get a good night's sleep. And if these suggestions don't help, there's a list of websites you can turn to which cover pretty much every eventuality - except your iPod getting run over by a bus. That's just careless.

!OUCH: My iPod's frozen. Like an Eskimo on a particularly nippy day
THERE, THERE: Try resetting your machine. Connect it to the AC adaptor, turn the Hold switch on and off and then hold down Menu and Select (Menu and Play on older white iPods) until you see the Apple logo. If you don't have the adaptor handy, the procedure should still work. Resetting doesn't get rid of your tunes, but you will lose your preferences and

personal settings, like your On-The-Go playlist.
If the iPod refuses to cooperate, leave it for
twenty-four hours without power to
completely drain the battery, then connect to
the AC adaptor and reset again. Still no joy? On
the older white iPods, reset as normal, but
when you see the logo, play finger Twister and
press all four buttons at once to force it to run
a Disc Scan. This could take up to thirty
minutes. When your iPod's had a good root
around inside and dusted itself off it'll show
you a symbol. Fingers crossed . . . A tick means
everything's A-OK, an exclamation mark in a
triangle means that it's found a problem but
will try to fix it the next time you reset, an
arrow means that it fixed the problem but that
you should download the latest iPod software
and restore your machine. But an exclamation
mark and a sad iPod icon is seriously bad news.
Start preparing yourself to go cold turkey –
you'll have to send your iPod off to get it fixed
(http://depot.info.apple.com/ipod).

! OUCH: It won't reset
THERE, THERE: Naughty boy. You'll have to
get tough, take drastic measures and restore
your iPod. If you can, make sure you've got
copies of all your non-music files on your computer (your music is safe in iTunes) because
restoring wipes it completely and reverts it to
the virginal state it was in when you first
bought it. Connect the iPod to your computer
and open up your installer CD or download a
new version of the updater from

www.apple.com/ipod/download. Click restore, then follow the instructions. Like you're in the army or something.

! OUCH: It's constantly crashing. Like an Eastern European airline.

THERE, THERE: Updating the iPod's system software should get you back behind the wheel and on the right road. Apple produces firmware updates two or three times a year - find out which version you're running under the About menu on your iPod, then go to www.apple.com/swupdates/ to see whether you've got the latest one. If not, close down iTunes and all other applications, make sure you've backed up all the files on your iPod and run the updater, which erases all the data on your machine.

! OUCH: My mini's making horrible crackly noises

THERE, THERE: You might encounter this if you've been carrying your iPod around in your jeans pocket or putting too much pressure on the case when attaching it to a belt clip or armband. Or the distortion might occur when you touch the area around the headphone jack. What's happened is that the copper pins that connect the insides of your iPod to the earbud socket have been damaged. In some cases this can happen quite quickly. There were rumours that Apple was using the mini drought in the first half of 2004 as an excuse to buy time to fix this problem. Prevent it happening to you by treating your mini with the love and affection it clearly deserves. Hey, it's only liddle after all. And try not to insert and remove the headphones too often. However, if you are cursed already, get in touch with Apple or the shop where you bought it and they should give you a new one. No problem.

! OUCH: The battery icon is full, but my iPod still won't play
THERE, THERE: It's a glitch and the little fella's playing tricks on you. Just charge it up.

! OUCH: My iPod never charges fully
THERE, THERE: Reset it, and then play it until it runs out of power completely. Then fully recharge using the power adaptor. It should now be giving you 100 per cent. Or in football-speak, 110 per cent.

! OUCH: My iPod starts skipping after less than twenty-five minutes
THERE, THERE: Well maybe it's just really happy that it's got such a fab owner! Try leaving it well alone when you're running - using shuffle, playing around with the menu and flipping between tracks will all run down the twenty-five minutes. Stop it and press play while you take a breather and the buffer will fill up again.

! OUCH: The touchwheel doesn't respond when I'm wearing gloves
THERE, THERE: Like, duh! The touchwheel works by recognizing an electrical charge from your finger. So it won't function if you're wearing

mittens or if you use a pen or summat. And take off all that bling bling - that chunky bracelet could be interfering.

! OUCH: Someone changed the language to Outer Mongolian or something
THERE, THERE: My, my, we do have hilarious friends, don't we? You can do this one with your eyes closed (almost). Press the Menu button five times until nothing on the screen changes. Select the third item down (fourth on the mini), then scroll through the options until you see Reset All Settings written in English. Click on it and then go to Reset.

! OUCH: The Apple logo on my iPod seems to have settled in for the long haul
THERE, THERE: Connect to your computer and when you see the logo, press Play and Select (or Fast Forward and Rewind on older white models) to force your iPod into Enable Disk Mode. You should get the Do Not Disconnect message and the iPod icon should show up on your desktop, but if not, restart the computer. Make sure you've backed up all your iPod files before restoring your iPod with the latest updater firmware.

! OUCH: My computer doesn't recognize the iPod
THERE, THERE: Unplug any other FireWire devices connected to your computer. Then check for dirt or dust in your iPod cable and make sure it's plugged in properly. If it's not recognizing

your iPod as a hard disk, make sure the battery is charged, then reset it and when you see the Apple logo, press Play and Select (or Fast Forward and Rewind on older white models) until you see the Do Not Disconnect message.

❗ OUCH: I can't get rid of the Do Not Disconnect message
THERE, THERE: Firstly, make sure the iPod's not in Enable Disk Mode. If it is, you should be able to unmount manually by clicking on the source icon and going to Eject in iTunes or moving it to the Trash. If this doesn't work, reset your iPod and try ejecting again. A final option would be to push your computer's Power Management Unit (PMU) reset button once with a pen.

❗ OUCH: My iPod and iTunes are out of sync
THERE, THERE: You may be missing the iPod kernel extension. Don't worry, it can happen to the best of us. If you can't find the file iPodDriver.kext on your computer's hard disk, either reinstall iTunes from the CD or open up the iTunes installer and find the actual installer for the kext. Now snap your heels together and salute your new kernel.

❗ OUCH: I've got a really old computer and haven't got much disk space
THERE, THERE: Er, persuade your parents to buy you a new computer? Failing that, it's a bit of a desperate measure, but you can delete tracks you've uploaded to the computer from the iTunes Music folder on your computer's

hard drive. The songs will remain in the library so you can transfer them to the iPod, but you won't be able to move them into playlists or change any info any more. But beggars can't be choosers, eh? If you've got a Mac, you can use an Applescript (don't ask, just enjoy) called Rip To iPod (free, www.malcolmadams.com/itunes) that copies tracks to your iPod as you import a CD into iTunes, then immediately deletes the file on your computer. Cool.

! OUCH: I can't eject a CD
THERE, THERE: Disconnect your iPod and restart the computer and, in future, if you've already got a CD in the drive, turn off the option to automatically start iTunes when you connect your iPod. Otherwise, it might be that you've got a dodgy CD. Some bought CDs are copy-protected so always check the case and if it has a warning like 'Will not play on PC/Mac', don't insert it into your drive as it could lock up your computer and even damage your machine. For a list of known bad CDs, check out www.fatchuck.com/z3.html or http://ukcdr.org/issues/cd/bad. If you've already got one stuck inside, try pushing the PMU reset button. If that doesn't work, you'll probably have to take your computer in to be serviced. Boo.

! OUCH: One track keeps jumping in iTunes and another one's got ! next to it. Plus I've got a CD that iTunes doesn't seem to want to read
THERE, THERE: Dear oh dear, we are feeling sorry for ourselves, aren't we? If the same song

always skips then it's corrupted. Trash it from your iTunes Music folder on your computer's hard drive (it's no good deleting it from a playlist or the library in iTunes - that's just a shortcut) and import it again. The exclamation mark means that it can't find the track and you'll have to drag and drop the original version back into iTunes again from your music folder. If your computer's having problems with audio CDs, unclick Use Error Correction in Edit>Preferences>Importing. Feeling any better?

! OUCH: I get a 'Not A Valid Library File' or 'Error-208 Cannot Open iTunes Music Library' message when I try to open iTunes
THERE, THERE: Move all your music files from the iTunes folder to the desktop and then use File>Export Song List under the File menu to save all your playlists (you have to do it individually) in XML format, also on the desktop. Close iTunes while you trash its music library and music library.xml, then open again and go to Add Folder To Library in the File menu and select the one you stored on the desktop. To restore playlists, go to Import in the File menu and bring them back one by one. What a palaver.

! OUCH: Help! I accidentally deleted my iTunes library. Can I reinstall the files from my iPod?
THERE, THERE: Apple have made sure that it's not immediately obvious how to do this because it's illegal to copy music. But we'll

make a special exception in your case. In Windows, it's actually a piece of cake. With icing on top. Hold down Ctrl/Alt/Shift as you remount your iPod and switch on Manually Manage Songs And Playlists. Go to My Computer on the desktop, and click on the iPod folder to open its hard disk. Then go to Tools>Folder Options>View>Show Hidden Files And Folders and . . . drum roll . . . abacadabra! Your tunes appear. Drag and drop them back into the iTunes Music folder. Mac users should hold down Command and Option as they connect and then have to download and run add-on software. Try the free iPod Viewer (www.versiontracker.com) or iPodRip (£5, www.thelittleappfactory.com), which not only allows you to automatically update iTunes with songs you've downloaded from a different Mac - it even rescues song ratings too. For which we give it a rating of five out of five.

! OUCH!: Someone stole my iPod
THERE, THERE: Can't really help on that one, except offer a shoulder to cry on. But as your iPod only contains copies of your music, at least you haven't lost any of your tunes. Hey, look on the bright side!

ASSAULT AND BATTERY
Those battery-life scare stories laid to rest

The iPod's rechargeable lithium-ion battery has come in for a whole heap of flak over its lifespan but fortunately these days there's no need to lose too much sleep over it. Owners of the original iPods complained that it died after a year and a half and that Apple wouldn't replace it - instead suggesting that you buy a new iPod. Twenty-something Brooklynites Casey and Van Neistat took matters into their own hands in November 2003 after the battery in Casey's 15GB model conked out. The brothers made a film called *iPod's Dirty Secret*, which shows the partners in crime spray painting Apple's silhouette posters with the slogan: 'iPod's unreplaceable battery lasts only eighteen months' to a soundtrack of Casey's actual telephone conversation with the Apple help desk.

So many thousands of people clicked on to see the film that the website couldn't handle the traffic. No matter, soon it was on the evening news all around the world, and, even weirder, eleven normally stuffy British MPs stopped blathering on about road humps and pressed PM Tony Blair to pass a motion ensuring that replacement batteries would be available at a fair price in this country. Presumably worried that they wouldn't be able to listen to their 'Royal Philharmonic Plays Steps' album any more.

However, it all turned out to be a waste of valuable tax-payers' time as Apple had already started a battery replacement scheme - it's just that the hapless help desk bod that Casey called hadn't known about it. And it wasn't a problem peculiar to iPods either - many portable devices like mobile phones use similar batteries, which all wear out after a certain period of time, depending on how much you use it. Which, in the case of our beloved iPods, is usually every hour God gives.

Your battery should last for twelve hours (eight on the mini and older white iPods) when fully charged and ought to take about 500-700 charges, which, if you rev it up every day, means it should last just under two years. However, every time you connect your iPod to the computer, it starts charging. There's nothing you can do about this apart from not hooking up unnecessarily - it's better to charge your iPod from the power adaptor. The battery should take about four hours to charge fully, but for those of you (read: all of us) who can't wait, it'll be up to about eighty per cent charged after one hour. You can't blow it up by overcharging, so it's perfectly fine to leave it juicing up overnight so you're ready to put those headphones in as soon as you wake up.

But however much love you show your iPod, your battery will eventually go to the big battery farm in the sky. You can still use your iPod, but only if it's attached to the power source, which isn't exactly the way nature intended. Never fear. Apple will fit your iPod with a new battery for £86 - that's like 12p for every time you've charged it. Or maybe you were really sensible and signed up to the AppleCare two-year insurance scheme for £59 (www.apple.com/support/ipod). If so, just whip your machine off to the nice people at Apple and they'll send you back a brand new one. In fact, in many cases they really *will* send you back a brand new iPod. Which is nice. So you just need to make sure you've stored all your music files, notes, contacts and calendar information in a safe, cosy place on your computer, ready to reload back on to the iPod when it plops back through the letterbox.

You can also get cheaper replacement batteries from other companies (check out www.everythingipod.co.uk, www.amazon.co.uk) and some even come with mini-screwdrivers, but you'll probably need to get someone who knows a little about electronics (and we're not talking about wiring a plug here) to help you fit it. Firstly, if you open up the iPod yourself, your year's warranty with Apple is ripped up. And yes, they will notice. Even if you stick it back together with Superglue. If you are going to attempt this complicated surgical procedure yourself, check out the instructions at www.ipodbattery.com/ ipodinstall.htm, where some nimble-fingered and selflessly brave souls have taken one apart for the benefit of iPod science. So we shouldn't use a hammer, then? We can't thank you enough, guys.

FIGHT THE POWER

How to get more oomph out of your battery

1. Always flip the Hold switch on when you're not using your iPod so it doesn't keep turning itself on in your bag like an over-excited puppy.

2. Charge using the power adaptor as opposed to your computer.

3. Don't let it run down all the way so it's completely empty. Even if you're not using your iPod, a fully charged machine will run out of power after two to four weeks as the operating system ticks away while it's asleep.

4. Don't use the backlight unnecessarily. You know, just save it for those times when you want to show it off. OK, stop showing off now.

5. Your battery will last longer if you just leave the iPod to its own devices. Once you start jumping around between songs, caning the Fast Forward and Rewind buttons, and playing around with EQs, you'll squeeze the life out of it and will have to head back home in silence to Mr Charger.

6. Be careful if you're using the Repeat function - wander out of the room and forget about it and your iPod will keep merrily playing away until it can't take any more.

7. Use only AAC and MP3 files and load up your iPod with tracks that are smaller than 9MBs so it won't have to keep accessing the hard drive.

8. If you're using a case, remove your iPod before you charge it as the bottom of the machine acts as a cooling surface. If it's covered up, your iPod will overheat like an Eskimo in the Sahara. On a particularly hot day.

9. Don't unhook your iPod when it's displaying the 'Do not disconnect'

message. You could wreak untold damage.

10. Your iPod is not waterproof. Keep it out of the bathroom otherwise both of you could come to a watery end.

PUMP UP THE VOLUME

The loudness (or rather, quietness) of the iPod has almost caused as much debate as the battery

All iPods sold in the UK have to stick to strict European rules. And because the French will only allow an output of 100 decibels on personal music players, we all have to suffer in (near) silence. *Sacré blue!* First the 100 Years War, then poncy subtitled art films and now this. Fortunately there are ways to get round the volume cap - so listen up, as it were. You could buy an iPod while on holiday in the US (where you'd get it cheaper too). But for those of us who wouldn't know an Air Mile if it fell out of the sky and hit us on the head, download a small free tool called euPod Volume Boost (Windows only, www.ipod-lounge.com) and run it each time you add new music files to iTunes. It's also rumoured that restoring your iPod with Software Updater 2.1 does the trick for white iPods, although it wipes the hard disk in the process. But be careful - don't crank it up too high because an iPod freed from its shackles can burst your eardrums. Hello? ARE YOU LISTENING? Oh, you must have done it already.

Where to go for more help

www.info.apple.com/usen/ipod/tshoot.html
Official Apple support pages

http://discussions.info.apple.com/webx/ipod
Apple's iPod discussion board

www.apple.com/support/itunes
Help with iTunes and iTunes Music Store

www.methodshop.com
Loads of trouble-shooting FAQs

www.macintouch.com/ipod.html
Check in for the latest postings

THIRD-PARTY SOFTWARE

If you're still in a spot of bother, some of the clever little programs on these websites might get you out of jail free:

> www.redchairsoftware.com/anapod
> www.apple.com/macosx/downloads
> www.ephpod.com
> www.ipodhacks.com
> www.ipodlounge.com
> www.macupdate.com
> www.mediafour.com
> www.versiontracker.com

APPLESCRIPTS

Ever wondered if you could manually delete an iPod playlist or sync your iTunes Play Count with that on your iPod? Discover the weird and wonderful world of shortcuts you never knew you needed for Mac users.

www.malcolmadams.com/itunes/index.php-
www.scriptbuilders.net

i'M a celebrity: Skateboard king Tony Hawk

'I love my iPod because it's a compact, intuitive and highly compatible device that can store a large musical library. I'd love an iPod with a bigger drive, though, somewhere in the fifty to a hundred GB range!'

i'M a celebrity: Tom Fletcher (McFly)

'I use it to listen to music in the car on the way to promotions, which is great because we're travelling quite a bit at the moment. It's made my bag loads lighter as I don't have to carry loads of CDs around. My most-played track is "Eleanor Rigby" by The Beatles. It looks cool too!'

iSay . . .

'I take my iPod travelling with me. I even use the back as a shaving mirror.' Ted Sealey, Sydney, Australia

'I use it at the gym to block out all the groaning men with weights!' Maria Bablumian, Surrey

TEST YOUR iQ

Take our iPod knowledge quiz. Answers opposite.

1. Where is the Apple HQ where the iPod was created?

2. What's the shortcut for turning the backlight on?

3. What did iPod designer Johnny Ives design before he joined Apple?

4. From which decade is Steve Jobs's favourite style of music?

5. What award did the iTunes software win?

6. Which celebs have lent their signature to limited-edition iPods?

7. Which superstar techno DJ played a set on iPods at the Apple store in New York?

8. The iPod has featured in at least seven films. Name five (one point for each one) . . .

9. What was the secret way to find the hidden Brick game on the old iPods?

10. Why do all blank CD-Rs have room for at least 74 minutes of music?

HOW DID YOU DO?

(1-5) No iDea
We know the iPod looks lovely and that, but you are actually supposed to turn it on

(6-9) iPlates
You've obviously been lost in music . . . for the last millennium

(10-14) iPod therefore I am
What can we say? We salute you. Hello? HELLO! Can't you take those earbuds out for a second?

Answers

1. Cupertino, California, USA
2. Press and hold down the Menu button
3. Toilet bowls
4. The sixties. That's why iTunes comes with a preloaded playlist
5. A Technical Grammy in 2002 for outstanding contributions to the music industry and recording field
6. Madonna, Beck and Tony Hawk
7. Richie Hawtin
8. *Elf* (a new iPod in its box), *Runaway Jury* (used to store evidence), *Agent Cody Banks* (one of his gadgets), *The Italian Job* (Charlie Theron's character has one), *Stuck On You* (used by Greg Kinnear), *Timeline* (mounted on the female archaeologist's belt) and *Kal Ho Na No* (the iPod's even made it into Hindi culture!)
9. Go to the About screen and hold down the middle button for a few seconds
10. Because the former boss of Sony was a classical music nut and insisted they were big enough to fit Beethoven's Ninth Symphony – 74 minutes and 42 seconds long

Talking 'bout a Revolution

WE'VE SEEN THE FUTURE. AND IT'S WHITE

The iPod was already way off the cool chart when the super-cute mini gave birth to a whole new generation of smitten fans. Then Apple crossed over into Microsoft-land for the first time with iTunes For Windows and yet more people saw the light. Further deals, like the one with computer giant Hewlett Packard, have made it even more Windows-compatible. Surely world domination is just around the corner?

But Apple bosses aren't going to just sit back and twiddle their scrolling thumbs. You can bet your most-played track that they've already got the next generation of iPods up their sleeves - or maybe even surgically inserted in their ears? So what is next? The smart money's on bigger hard disks and smaller iPod. There have been rumours about a 2GB Very Mini for ages, but can we have both at the same time please? And no doubt Apple will bow to Podders' demands for the little pleasures in life, like being able to manually delete songs, DJ mixing software and the ability to play WMA files (the iPod already has the capacity apparently, it's just disabled right now).

Apple must also have taken note of its rivals' so-called 'iPod killers'. While they've had about as much impact as a fly swat on a swarm of locusts, some have a few features that could be incorporated. The Creative Jukebox Zen Xtra has a 60GB memory and 16 hours of battery life, as does the Rio Nitrus in a tiny 1.5GB player, while the Sony Hi-MD MiniDisc player lasts for a whopping fifty hours. You could forget to switch it off, come back two days later and it'd still be playing. Then there's the Cowon iAudio M3, which lets you record directly from your hi-fi/CD player, has a built-in voice recorder *and* an FM radio.

And what about other functions, apart from playing music? Apple has always managed to keep schtum about its next move (no MI5-style official-secrets leaks here), so iPod websites are a hotbed of rumours. Even before the mini was announced there were stories of a colour screen for viewing photos, a digital camera and a video player, perhaps for Quick-time film clips. The argument went that as you can already watch movie trailers through iTunes, the natural next step would be to transfer them to your iPod. Other companies such as Archos, RCA and Creative Lab already make portable players and you can now watch video on your mobile - some phones can show entire episodes of *Friends*. Which is always handy when your nan's on the other end of the line waffling on about the people from No 23 again. However, Apple's Steve Jobs has gone on record saying he thinks the iPod screen is too small and reckons that people don't use video in the same way as music - while we might watch a DVD three or four times, we'll play our favourite song over and over and never get bored.

What's more likely is that we'll see new ways of accessing, buying and transferring digital music files, so that buying albums the traditional way will become ancient history. Virgin Megastore plans to install consoles for downloading unrestricted MP3s straight to portable players and CDs in all its record shops as well as fast downloads direct to mobile phones. You could then play these MP3s wherever and however you like, either through mobile Internet access to your music library or by making unlimited copies. 'We're going to take digital music into the stratosphere,' reckons Virgin supremo Sir Richard Branson.

BskyB is hoping that soon we'll be able to download any song we're watching on a music channel directly to our set-top box through the telly, and then transfer it to a computer or digital player. Even old-skool stuffy libraries are getting in on the act - in Richmond in Surrey you can already borrow audio books while in Japan, libraries lend singles and albums on CD just three days after their release. Surely the next step is to do the same with copy-protected MP3s, possibly with in-built software licences that expire after thirty days so it's just like borrowing a book.

Meanwhile wireless Bluetooth technology will make it even easier for us to transfer data and music files between computers, phones and, hopefully, iPods. Accessories firm XtremeMac has said it will sell the first Bluetooth add-on for iPods in 2005 - wireless headphones. The device will allow you to ditch those famous white earbuds, tuck your iPod in your bag or drawer and control your music through a remote on the special headphones. Presumably in the future you will be able to use similar technology to beam music - not to mention text files and digital photos - between your iPod and a computer, or even to your friend's iPod.

With so many different machines able to talk to each other, the possibilities are endless. You could be out having a coffee, for example, hear a new tune you like, use your mobile to dial up a special music library that recognizes the song

 and allows you to buy it. You could then download it to your phone and beam it wirelessly to your iPod. How's that for a digital music revolution?

Now if you don't mind, we're off to listen to our 'Thank God We've Finished The Book' playlist . . .

i'M a celebrity: Moby

'*I can't imagine music any other way. I can be on an aeroplane and think to myself, "Wouldn't you like to listen to the first Roxy Music record?" And there it is.*'

iSay . . .

'Every year I'd have to buy a new CD player because it'd break or I'd get sand in it on holiday. But I've had my iPod for three years and it still works perfectly. I'm never going to have to buy another music player again.' Raj Panjwani, London

'I saw a fifty-year-old farmer dude with a huge beard and an iPod tucked into the pocket of his overalls. I thought, "Wow these things are getting out of control."' Van Williams, Colarado, US

'The iPod's turned me into a real music junkie - now I have my tunes anywhere and everywhere. I would truly miss my iPod if I had to give it up. Tears would flow.' Kenny Lewis, Kettering